# PRACTICAL

# COMPUTER

# EDUCATION

## FOR CAMEROON COLLEGES

BY

### CONI T. TAWONG

# TOBBY VISION COMPUTERS Ltd

Practical Computer Education

First Edition 2011

© 2011, Cornelius Tfurndabi Tawong.

Bamenda-Cameroon.

**ISBN 9956-639-57-5**

Typescript, Cover design and Layout by
Tobby Vision Computers Ltd Bambui
**Email:** corneliustawong@yahoo.com
corneliustawong@gmail.com
tobbyvision@yahoo.com

P. O. Box 309 Bamenda - Cameroon

Printing by Gospel Press Bamenda

**DEDICATION**

**This Book Is Dedicated To:**

**My late grandfather**
**NGWANG KUMANTA MUNKI**

**&**

**CAROL HISHON**

Each of them now peacefully resting with the Lord.

# FOREWORD

The approach of the author of this book indicates a keen recognition of the present day needs and interest of students enrolled or who wish to enroll in microcomputer studies. He has touched the lives of other students and given direction, inspired, and enriched their lives.

He has also lighted a candle in the lives of others which has become an external light inspiring men and women everywhere to reach for a star in computer studies.

We must realize that the development of every person depends directly or indirectly on the development of all persons. It is my hope that this book contributes in some small way to the broadening of other peoples' perspectives that leads to better understanding of the contemporary problems in computer studies.

Finally it is a challenge to meet the needs of all students in all aspects of computer studies. Good luck if you are able to afford a copy for yourself.

**Dr. Vunan Vugar Paul**
**Ph.D (Education)**

# SPECIAL THANKS

My gratitude to my lovely wife Tfurndabi Mangoh Yinike of ENIET Mbengwi for the many hours she spent encouraging me in bringing this manuscript into a readable form.

Special appreciation to my brother Mr. George, Wendi Kwison of GBHS Bamenda whose support and encouragement were constantly felt.

I want to express my sincere gratitude to my mother, brothers and sisters for their wonderful love.

I also want to thank friends and classmates for their advice in preparing this book. I am particularly grateful to Mr. Ngong Alfred Targha computer science teacher from ENS Yaounde, Mr. Tume Erasmus Computer Science teacher Saint Augustine's College Nso, Mrs Nkwate Vera Mbaya of PPN Computer Systems Bamenda – the lady who put so much data base skills into my being. Also thanks to Dr. Nick Ngwanyam of St. Louis University Institute Bamenda for the observations and criticisms he made to this work.

I owe a great debt of gratitude to Prof. & Mrs Anthony Ndi of Foncha Street Bamenda who gave me the first impression of computers and Rev. Fr. John Willeit of Bressanone – Italy who bore the entire financial study burden with persevering love. Every once in a long while the world is blessed by the presence of a soul such as Willeit. I am doubly blessed to be able to call him my friend.

And with great humility, my eternal gratitude to Rev. Mgr. Ronald Hishon, Short Close, Poole, Dorset England who made it possible for this book to be published. I thank Pa Bonu C. Barnabas for providing me with pictures of "Atsam", "Mbomaya" hill and one of the late fons of Bambui. Also many thanks to my students especially Eusebia, Solange, Mary, Melvis, Genesis and Numfor whose pictures I have used and who worked with me to produce this book.

Lastly I thank all the people of Bambui where I have lived for the past seven years. A people so blessed with all it takes to know and love God. I cannot forget my wonderful people of Tabenken and Dr. Robert Pool of Amsterdan – Holland whose studies on Medical Anthropology of these good people made me recognize how God endowers some of these simple people with astonishing knowledge.

# Table of Contents

## CHAPTER ONE

## CHAPTER TWO

### MICROSOFT WINDOWS OPERATING SYSTEM

## CHAPTER THREE

## WORD PROCESSING

**CHAPTER FOUR**

## INTERNET

## What is a Computer?

A computer is a fast and accurate electronic device functioning under the control of instructions stored in its own memory, can accept data, and process the data into useful information that is displayed before the user and can be stored for future use.

Data refers to text, numbers, words, audio, video sent to a computer during the input operation. Information refers to data processed into a form that has meaning and is useful.

Basically, a computer performs the following tasks:

- Input (sending data to the computer is known as input)
- Processing (work done by the computer to produce results)
- Storage (place to store results from processing)
- Output (result displayed by computer)

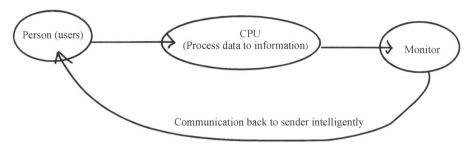

Generally, a computer is not a single device. A computer is made up of several devices that function together as a system. Examples of devices that make up a computer include; Monitor, Motherboard, CPU(Microprocessor), Main memory, Expansion cards, Power supply unit, Optical discs drive, Hard disk drive (HDD), Keyboard, Mouse, Printer, Scanner, Speakers, DVD drive, Digital camera, Microphone, Modem, CD burner, DVD burner etc.

**Why Study Computers?**

Today many people believe that knowing how to use a computer is a basic skill necessary to succeed in business or to function effectively in society. It is important to understand that while computers are used in many different ways, there are certain types of common application software that computer users need to know. It is this type of software that you will learn how to use during your computer use course with this book. Given the widespread use and availability of computer systems, knowing how to use common application software on a computer system is an essential skill practical for everyone.

## How the Computer Works

Mastering the theory and principle on which any piece of equipment or machine works is the basis in understanding the techniques of use and maintenance. A simplified way of understanding how the computer works is to know what goes into the computer (which is data); what comes out of it (which is information) and to understand the process of converting data into information (which is data processing). The following steps summarises the process of how a computer works.

- **Input**
- **Processing /Storage**
- **Output**

**Input:** Sending data to the computer is known as input. Input devices are the keyboard, trackball, touch pad, printing stick (used to move pointer and select options or objects), joy stick (used for games), light pen (used to select options and draw on the screen), graph table (used to enter or edit drawings), scanners (converts texts, graphics or pictures into digital input) format understood by the computer e.g. optical character recognition (OCR) using light source to read codes, marks, characters and digits), digital cameras (captures digital images of objects), microphone (send sound to the computer) etc.

As we type on the keyboard, we are generating electrical signals which bear specific codes in the hexadecimal mode (hexadecimal mode is a system of numbering based on 16 digits that is often used for graphics also called base 16 number system). These digits are 0, 1, 2, 3, 4, 5, 6, 7, 8, 9, A, B, C, D, E and F. A stands for 10, B for 11, C for 12, D for 13, E for 14 and F for 15. These codes are subsequently interpreted as characters and symbols. Function keys (F1-F12 on the keyboard see keyboard on Figure 1) and sometimes the combination of two or three keys can issue a specialised command.

The keyboard uses a system which gives each key a unique electrical pulse. The key board basic input output system (BIOS) recognises and translates the code an eight binary bit (digital bit). This is then forwarded to the central processing unit (CPU) for processing.

**Processing:** It is work done by the computer processor to produce results. The processor is a very complicated circuit chip [logic circuits] which is built with millions of logic gates. These logic gates use and compare digital signals (binary digits). Binary digits consist of two digits and also known as the base two numbering system. In order to think human beings use an organ called the brain. The "thinking" in computers is done by a component known as the processor. Thus, the processor is the hardware device that interprets and executes commands of a stored program in the computer. Computer processors exist in different forms. A personal computer has only one processing chip called the microprocessor or central

20

processing unit (CPU). A microcomputer with a Pentium IV processor is called a Pentium IV computer. Microprocessors are manufactured by companies like Intel Corporation, AMD, Motorola and Cyrix. Microcomputers are generally named after the type of CPU they contain. The performance of a processor is measured in terms of the speed with which it executes its operations. This speed is called the clock frequency and is measured in Hertz (Hz) or Giga Hertz (GHz). Modern processor speeds exceed 1.5GHz or 2.1GHz. The high speed CPUs usually generate a lot of heat and need to be cooled. The devices that are commonly used for reducing the temperature of the CPU are the CPU heat sink with fan and the system fan. If a CPU is not sufficiently cooled, it may develop functional problems or it can even stop working.

The CPU consists of five main sections; the arithmetic logic unit (ALU), control unit, cache, buses, and a set of registers. The functions of the CPU are to:

- Carry out arithmetic operations;
- Carry out logical operations; and
- Control all devices connected to the Personal Computer (PC).

**Storage:** Storage is a place to store results inside or outside the computer. Storage devices are hardware devices that hold computer data. The total amount of data that can be held on storage devices is called the storage capacity of the device.

Basic Input Output System (BIOS) is built-in program, which keeps track of all devices attached to the computer and acts as an inter–communication channel between these devices. Older computers contained read only BIOS (Basic Input Output System) that could not be altered. This limited the user's ability to upgrade their computers. So Flash BIOS was introduced. Now when a new component is installed in the computer, the Flash BIOS can be electronically upgraded so that it can recognize and communicate with the new devices.

The BIOS is placed in a Read Only Memory (ROM) chip that comes with the computer (it is often called a ROM BIOS). This ensures that the BIOS will always be available and will not be damaged by disk failures. It also makes it possible for a computer to boot [boot refers to the computer starting up process when the configuration files are loaded into memory] itself. As Random Access Memory (RAM) is faster than ROM, therefore many computer manufacturers design systems for copying the BIOS from ROM to RAM each time the computer is booted. This is known as **shadowing.**

Storage capacity is measured in bytes, kilobytes (KB), megabytes (MB), gigabytes (GB) etc. A byte of information can be 11001100 or 0011 1101.

1 byte = 8 bits

1 kilobyte (Kb) = 1.024 bytes

1 megabyte (MB) = 1.048.576 bytes

1 gigabyte (GB) = 1.073.741.824 bytes

1 terabyte (TB) = 1.099.511.627.776 bytes

1 petabyte (PB) = 1.125.899.906.842.624 bytes

1 exabyte (EB) = 1.152.921.504.606.846.976 bytes

The term **memory** stands for storage that comes in the form of chips, and the term **storage** is used for memory that exists on tapes or disk. Memory is usually used as short reference for physical memory, related with actual chips. The word 'main' added to the computer's memory distinguishes it from external mass storage devices like floppy disks, compact discs and memory sticks. Besides the main memory, your computer also has a physical temporary internal storage place. That place is known as Random Access Memory or RAM. We can compare ROM to text printed on paper and RAM is like text written on dust so you can copy text from paper to dust but when wind blows the text wipes itself so data you write on dust stays only when there is no wind. RAM is the place in a computer where the operating system (program or software which help start up the computer), application (software used to create things) programs, and data in current use are kept so that they can be quickly accessed by the computer's processor. RAM is faster to read from and write to than other kinds of storage devices in your computer. However, data stays in RAM only as long as your computer is running like data copied from paper onto dust stays only when there is no wind. When you turn the computer off, RAM loses its data. When you turn on your computer again, the operating system and other files are once again loaded into RAM, usually from the hard disk. In other words, we can say that RAM is volatile (memory that loses the data when the computer is turned off).

There are two types of RAM, **Static RAM (SRAM)** and **Dynamic RAM (DRAM).** Dynamic RAM must be constantly refreshed (re–energized) or it will lose its contents. Static RAM (SRAM) does not need to be refreshed and is faster and more reliable than DRAM. Extended Data Out RAM (EDO RAM) is an improved version of Dynamic RAM (DRAM). EDO RAM can perform more than one task at a time.

Read Only Memory or ROM is built in computer memory containing data that normally can only be read, not written to. ROM contains the programming that allows your computer to "boot up" or regenerate each time you turn it on. Unlike RAM the data in ROM is not lost when the computer power is turned off. ROM is sustained by a small life–long battery in your computer. ROM chip that stores instructions or data is referred to as a firmware. Firmware is therefore the combination of software and hardware.

Besides computers, ROMs are used extensively in calculators and peripheral devices such as laser printers, whose fonts are often stored in ROMs. A variation of ROM is PROM (programmable read–only memory). PROM is a memory chip on which data can be written only once. A program written on PROM remains there forever. The difference between PROM and ROM is that PROM is manufactured as blank memory, whereas ROM is programmed during the manufacturing process. A type of PROM is EPROM (Erasable Programmable Read Only Memory). EPROM can be erased and re–used. Erasure is caused by an intense ultraviolet light through a window that is designed into the EPROM chip.

**Output devices:** There are two main kinds of output – soft copy and hard copy. Soft copy is information that is displayed on the computer screen or stored as files on a storage device. Hard copy is information that is printed on paper. Examples of computer output devices are the monitors (soft output), printers, speakers, plotters (hard output) devices.

**Computer Systems**

Basically, there are about six (6) basic types of computer systems in common usage:

**Supercomputer** – Is the fastest and the most expensive computer. Its huge processing power means it can be used for complex applications such as weather forecasting and detection of decryptions. Features include; it is used in science and engineering, thousand of processors, 10.000.000.000 (ten trillion) calculations per second, expensive – the cost about 100 million pounds (7.940.000francs CFA).

**Mainframe**. It comes second to super computer. It has the following features; it is larger in size compared to other computers; have large capacity and is more powerful in terms of processing speed.

**Server**. It is similar to the mainframe in that it serves many uses with the main difference that the users (called clients) do their own processing usually. The server processes are devoted to sharing files and managing log on rights. A server is a central computer that contains collections of data and programs. Also called a network server, this system allows all connected users to share and store electronic data and applications. Two important types of servers are file and application servers.

**Workstation**. Workstations are high-end, expensive computers that are made for more complex procedures and are intended for one user at a time. Some of the procedures consist of science, mathematics and engineering calculations and are useful for computer design and manufacturing. Workstations are sometimes improperly named for marketing reasons. Real workstations are not usually sold in retail.

**The Personal Computer (PC) or Microcomputer**. Single person use of a computer system in interactive mode for extended duration. The introduction of microprocessors, a single chip with all the circuitry that formerly occupied large cabinets, led to the proliferation of personal computers. Its physical characteristics and low cost are appealing and useful for its users. The capabilities of a personal computer have changed greatly since the introduction of electronic computers. Within a personal computer you have Monitor, Motherboard, CPU (Microprocessor), Main memory, Expansion cards, Power supply unit, Optical disc drive, Hard disk drive (HDD), Keyboard, Mouse, etc.

**Minicomputer or Microcontroller**. It enables the user to store data, do simple commands and tasks, with little or no user interaction with the processor. Many such systems are known as embedded systems. Examples of embedded systems include **smart phones** or car safety systems. Mini computers are important; they are used every day in devices such as appliances and automobiles.

**History and Evolution of Computers**

The term computer has evolved through history, resulting from man's attempt to create tools that would help him manipulate data effectively and efficiently. Each stage of change adds a function to the task performed by the previous development in this concept, giving a different definition to the term computer. It was necessary to calculate and analyze tasks employing the use of a machine. Many scientists have tried this. The seed of modern computer was sown 3500 years ago when a huge stone carved structure spread in circular pattern over the huge ground was used to perform astronomical calculations by considering the position of sun rays. This stone-carved structure is known as Neolithic Computer and is the oldest computer found till date.

Figure 2: Abacus

Figure 3: Stone Henge

The Abacus is a calculating instrument used by Chinese, Japanese and Koreans since ancient times. It was used in business as well as in scientific areas such as astronomical calculations, trigonometric calculations etc.

In 1642, the French mathematician Blaise Pascal invented a machine, which he called Numerical Wheel Calculator. Later the Numerical Wheel Calculator became popular as

**Pascaline.** Although this was a remarkable achievement it had a few draw backs:

Figure4: Blaise Pascal                    Figure 5: Pascaline

In 1673 the German philosopher mathematician Gottfried Leibnitz built a mechanical calculating machine that multiplies, divides, adds and subtracts faster than Pascaline. Arithmetic capability is one of the prime functions performed by a computing device. The real beginning of computers as we know them today started with the efforts of English mathematics professor Charles Babbge. In 1821, Babbage invented a machine known as the **Difference Engine** to perform mathematical calculations. In 1832, he got an idea to develop another machine that could perform not only mathematical tasks but also any type of calculation.

Figure 6: Charles Babbage          Figure 7: Difference Engine

Soon, he began work on the new machine, and in 1856 he succeeded in developing it. The new machine was named the **Analytical Engine.** Due to his contribution in the field of computers, Charles Babbage is also known as father of modern computers.

Three American scientists – John von Neumann, Eckert and Mauchly – jointly developed the Electronic Numerical Integrator and Calculator (ENIAC) on February 19, 1946. They were commissioned by the US army ordinance department for military reasons during World War II. This project began in 1943. It was put to work on calculation for atomic bomb research at LOS Alamos, New Mexico Government Research Laboratory. ENIAC was less impressive because it needed a large amount of electric power to run, weighed some thirty tons, very large with each operation controlled by different programs which could not be stored internally as in modern computers and to change from one computer to another difficult.

1n 1945, the Hungarian born mathematician John Von Neuman wrote a brilliant report describing several hardware concepts and that of stored programs. With the stored program concept, the instructions for the computer are coded and stored in the machine. Electrical signals or pulses that bear specific codes in the hexadecimal coded (see glossary) mode are subsequently interpreted as characters and symbols.

In 1947, he defined that computer as "a device that accepts input, process data, and stores information and produces output." The Electronic Discrete Variable Automatic Computer which Von helped invent was the first to use the stored program concept.

Mauchly and Eckert designed the Universal Automatic Computer being the first commercially available electronic digital computer.

It was introduced in 1951 and the first one delivered to the US census bureau to tabulate census statistics. It was used to predict the 1952 US Presidential elections. Public awareness of computers increased when in 1952 the UNIVAC after analyzing only 5 percent of the tallied votes, correctly predicted that Dwight D. Eisenhower would win the Presidential elections.

The first commercialized computers were purely used for research and database management purposes. However, as the transistor industry began making chips which could replace very large circuits, cheaper and less cumbersome computers began to surface.

The first Personal Computer or Microcomputer was introduced in 1981 by International Business Machines (IBM). IBM branded it the PC8086. Since then the PC has evolved from 80186, 80286, 80386, 80486, 80586, 80686 nowadays called Pentium II, Pentium III, Pentium IV, Pentium D etc. However during this period another computer company was also in existence and undergoing different evolutionary branding. The Machintosh family of computers at the time was incompatible to the IBM compatible computers both in hardware and software. The IBM compatibles have however won popularity. So learning how to use a computer with this book will be based on IBM compatible computers.

Though the two companies are different, the overall picture of their computers in terms of structure and functions is the same.

**Computer Hardware:** Refers to the physical elements of a computer. Also referred to as the machinery or the equipment of the computer. Examples of hardware are the keyboard, the monitor, the mouse and the processing unit. However, part of a computer's hardware cannot be seen; in other words, it is not an external element of the computer, but rather an internal one, surrounded by the computer's casing. A computer's hardware is comprised of many different parts, but perhaps the most important of these is the motherboard.

In contrast to software, hardware is a physical entity, while software is non-physical entity. Hardware and software are interconnected, without software; the hardware of a computer would have no function. However, without the creation of hardware to perform tasks directed by software via the central processing unit, software would be useless.

**Computer Software:** Commonly known as programs, consist of all electronic instructions that tell the hardware how to perform a task. These instructions come from a software developer in the form that will be accepted by the operating system that they are based on. For example, a program that is designed for the Windows operating system will only work for that operating system. Compatibility of software will vary as the design of the software and the operating system differ. Software can also be described as a collection of routines, rules and symbolic languages that direct the functioning of the hardware.

Software is capable of performing specific tasks, as opposed to hardware which only perform mechanical tasks that they are mechanically designed for. Practical computer systems divided software systems into three major classes:

**System Software:** Consist of all the programs, languages and documentation supplied by the computer manufacturer. System software (programs) allow the application developers to write and develop their own programs. An important part of system software is the operating system, device drivers (sound card driver, display driver), viruses, diagnostic tools and more. Today many computers use an operating system that has a Graphical User Interface (GUI) that provides visual clues such as icons and symbols to help the user. Microsoft Windows 95/98/2000/XP/Vista/7/8, Mac, Linux are widely used graphical operating systems. DOS (disk operating system) is an older but still widely used operating system that is only text based.

**Programming Software:** Software that assists programmers in writing computer programs or applications.

**Application Software:** Allows users to accomplish one or more tasks. The different ways people use computers in their careers or in their personal lives, are examples of types of application software.

**Firmware:** Is a programme for hardware. It is an embedded coded program for the hardware. So it can perform its function specifically for which device it is made. Every device has inbuilt firmware. That gives the device the ability to perform its work. There are a lot of devices that use a screen and a button. The device consists of firmware that instructs the device to perform certain functions on given commands. Examples are a video and sound card.

## Categories Of Application Programs

**Word Processing Software:** The key advantage of word processing software is that it allows users to create, edit a document. Users can easily make changes in a document such as correcting errors of spellings and grammar, changing margins, adding, deleting or reallocating entire paragraphs. These changes will be difficult and time consuming to make using manual methods such as with the typewriter. With a word processor a document can be printed easily and easily stored on a disk for future reference. Programs here are oriented towards working with text but most word processor packages can also include numeric and graphic information. Word processors allow you to create things like; simple letters, reports, manuals, newsletters, fax messages, banners, brochures, etc.

Examples of word processors: Microsoft Word, Word Pad, Word Perfect etc.

**Electronic Spread Sheet Software:** Allows the user to add, subtract, and perform user defined calculations on rows and columns of numbers. These numbers can be changed and the spreadsheet quickly recalculates the new result. It eliminates the tedious recalculation required with manual methods. Spreadsheet information frequently is converted into a graphic form. Graphic capabilities are included in most spreadsheet packages. Examples are Microsoft Excel, Lotus 1–2–3, Lotus WordPro or Corel Word Perfect etc.

**Database Software:** Are useful for storing, sorting and retrieving large amounts of data. Invoices or orders, which may be in large numbers, can be managed better by using a database program. It also allows you to add new information, search through previously stored data, and print records. An organization, for example, might require a database about its various products, suppliers, employees, and customers. Most widely used database programs are Microsoft Access, MySQL, Oracle etc.

**Presentation Graphics Software:** Includes creation, modification, reformatting and printing of presentation materials. Allow users to create visual presentations. Examples are Microsoft Power Point, Ulead Photo Express etc.

**Multimedia Software:** Allows users to create modify and present images, audio, video etc. Example: Real Player, Media Player etc.

**Desktop Publishing Software:** Allow users to publish marketing literature, magazines, books and design cards. Examples: Microsoft Publisher, Adobe PageMaker, Adobe Illustrator, CorelDRAW, Print Artist, Photo Shop etc.

**Computer Aided Design Software:** Computer Aided Design (CAD) is a technique that enables engineers and manufacturers to make basic designs of their products on a computer. CAD packages help engineers to create and analyze the design of a product thoroughly before its actual manufacture. Topics include orthographic projections, section drawings, auxiliary projection, dimensioning, isometric drawings and assembly drawings. Examples: AutCAD, DeltaCAD, AchiCAD, Max etc.

**Accessories:** These are programs that come along with the operating system and enable users to type, design and to have fun and entertainment with the computer. Example: Notepad, Paint, Solitaire, CD Player etc.

**Web Browsers:** Used to view, download, upload, surf, or otherwise access documents (for example, Web pages) on the Internet. Example: Internet Explorer, Netscape Navigator, Mozilla Firefox etc.

**Commercial Software:** Installation in number of computers is specified by the software vendor/producer. Users only buy the license to use it. Users do not buy the software. He/she may not be allowed to install software on more than one machine.

**Shareware:** May be free of charge or the software company may charge a nominal fee. Users can download these kinds of software from the Internet. Example: Real Player full version, MP3 player full version, different games downloaded from the internet.

**Freeware:** Software that are given away for free by the vendor/producer. Example: Real Player trial version, MP3 Player trial version etc.

Computers for personal use (see Personal or Microcomputers page 6) come in all shapes and sizes, from the tiny Personal Digital Assistant (PDA) to the hefty Personal Computer towers, Handheld Personal Computers (HPC), Palmtop Personal Computers (PPC), Tablet Personal Computers, Laptops, Desktop, Mini tower, Notebooks etc. More specialised models are announced each week. Students, trip planners, accountants, language translators, teachers, businessmen etc should check for most recent models. When talking about Personal Computers (PCs) most people probably think of the desktop type which are designed to sit on the desk. The Mini tower and smaller mini tower style cases have become popular as people need more room for extra drives inside. Students certainly appreciate the mini tower types for the more space inside for all the cables and circuit boards and their knockles.

Before proceeding, let us have in mind that Computer Science refers to the study of computers and how they can be used, Computer literate means to be able to use computers well. The act of using computers is known as computing. The set of technological tools used to communicate, create, disseminate, store and manage information which include computers, Internet, broadcasting (radio and television) and telephony are referred to as the Information and Communication Technologies (ICTs).

# GLOSSARY CHAPTER ONE

**Application** also called a program; software designed for end users that helps the computer do specific activities such as Word processing or spreadsheets.

**Byte** – A unit of measure of computer memory. A byte generally represents one character, such as "A," and is made up of eight bits.

**Browser** – A program that allows a user to find, view, hear, and interact with material on the World Wide Web.

**CD–ROM** – A device that can read information from a CD.

**Computer** – A machine that processes data, which can be in the form of words, numbers, or graphics, and can help organize, edit, and file information.

**Data:** Refers to text, numbers, words, audio, video sent to a computer during the input operation.

**Database**: A software program used to organize, find, and display information in many different ways; any organized collection of information on a given subject or topic.

**Disk drive**: A machine that reads data from and writes data onto disk.

**External storage media:** External devices such as peripheral hard drives, DVD drives, flash drives, or memory card readers.

**Firefox:** An Internet browser developed by Mozilla.

**Function keys:** The keys F1–F12 on the keyboard.

**Hard drive:** A permanent storage device, usually a stack of disks enclosed in a computer case; used to store large amounts of information; often called the "C" drive.

**Hardware:** The mechanical devices that comprise a computer system, such as the central processing unit, monitor, keyboard, and mouse, as well as other equipment like printers and speakers.

**Home keys:** The keys A, S, D, F, J, K, L, and ; on the keyboard.

**Keyboard:** An input device that allows for communication with computer; include letters, numbers, symbols, and function keys.

**Keys:** The buttons on a keyboard.

**Laptop:** A portable computer.

**Memory:** Temporary computer information storage which is emptied when you turn off the computer; also called RAM.

The term "memory" also refers to the physical chips capable of holding data.

**Monitor**  A display screen and the box that contains it

**Mouse** A palm-size device attached to a computer by a cord, which allows the user to select items displayed on the screen by controlling the cursor, and to give commands by clicking the device's buttons. (See also "Hardware")

**Numeric keypad:** The keypad that allows you to type numbers when the Num Lock key is on.

**Program:** Software that helps the computer do specific activities; an organized list of instructions written in a special language.

**RAM:** random access memory: A computer component that allows you to store data.

**Removable media:** Storage media, such as a CD, DVD, or flash drive, which can be taken away from your PC.

**Screen:** Short for display screen; the display part of a monitor.

**Software:** A computer program, which provides the instructions which enable the computer hardware to work. System software, such as Windows or Mac OS, operate the machine itself, and applications software, such as spreadsheet or word processing programs, provide specific functionality.

**Window** Enclosed rectangular space on a computer screen, often used on our site to refer to the browser window for the display of a website.

**Windows XP/7** A system program that help to start up the computer and manages the hardware resources of the computer (see also operating system).

41

# CHAPTER TWO

## MICROSOFT WINDOWS OPERATING SYSTEM

Windows Operating System help to start up the computer controls it hardware and interpret the instructions from software and itself to the hardware. Desktop shortcuts look the same as they did in previous windows operating systems. If you are familiar with the Internet and have *surfed* the World Wide Web, you will recognize that shortcuts have become hyperlinks. Links appear within a web page as coloured text, pictures or buttons. When you click on a link, you jump to the page the link points to. Many other features which make one version of Windows Operating system different from the other is noticed after using several Windows Operating Systems.

When using a menu command such as File, Save, the operating system is the driving force that writes the file to our disk or hard disk. It includes the ability to run more than one program at a time (multitasking). Microsoft Windows uses a **Graphical User Interface (GUI).** This is a screen that appears when you start a computer, containing all the choices available to you. It allows you run through the use of pictures and graphics instead of typing out long commands to the operating system as the case with Disk Operating System.

## Starting Windows

To start windows, you turn on your system unit and monitor. As your computer boots, windows loads the files it needs to run. After the operating system is loaded, you may see a password dialog box asking for your username and password. The username and password is provided by the network administrator to the members of the network. You should use the same username and password each time you log onto windows so that your desktop, application programs and customization settings will always remain the same. By default windows displays a log on dialog box if you are on a network or have a network card attached to your computer.

Figure 2.1: **Windows Desktop**

After windows starts, you will see various items on the screen which will enable you to open applications, manage files and send receive emails and perform many other tasks throughout your work day. Depending on your installation, you may or may not see all of the items. Upgrading from a previous version of windows you may see additional icons on your desktop. The common components on windows screen include:

**Desktop** – This is the background on which all other elements appear. Think of it as your own traditional office desk. Just as you can move papers around, hide certain items in drawers and add remove things on your desk, you can manipulate items on your windows desktop.

**Icons –** Are pictures that represent programs (Microsoft Word, Microsoft Excel, Microsoft PowerPoint) etc, folders, files, printer information, computer information, and so on in both Windows and programs designed to run under windows. Most often you use icons to open folders and files.

**Task bar** – contains the start button and any open applications and the time. You can click the task bar button to open the window or the application it represents. Use the start button to open programs, documents, get help and support and so on.

**Pointer** – It is an onscreen icon that represents your mouse or other selecting device. You use it to select items and choose commands.

**Boot** – Used to describe a computer starting up process during which the operating system and configuration files are loaded into the computer memory.

**Username and Password** – identifies you to your computer or the network server and protects your computer from illegal entry.

**Log on** – Attaching to the computer network so you can use it resources like printers, scanners etc. In order to avoid error messages at logon, make sure you type the password correctly and use the appropriate case when typing. Pressing Enter in a dialog or message box is the same as choosing the Ok button. Pressing the Esc (Escape) key is the same as choosing the Cancel button.

**What's is This?** – A Windows XP tool that helps you to know what happens when you activate a check box. If you are using Windows XP, click on start button, point to Settings, select Taskbar and Start Menu to go to the Taskbar and Start menu Properties dialog box. Right click on the Show Clock check box and click on What's is This?

A message comes up explaining what would happen if you activate the check box. You will use this feature in windows operating system and application programs to understand what happens when certain options are activated or deactivated.

Figure 2.2. below: **Study of some of the common icons on Windows Desktop.**

| | |
|---|---|
| 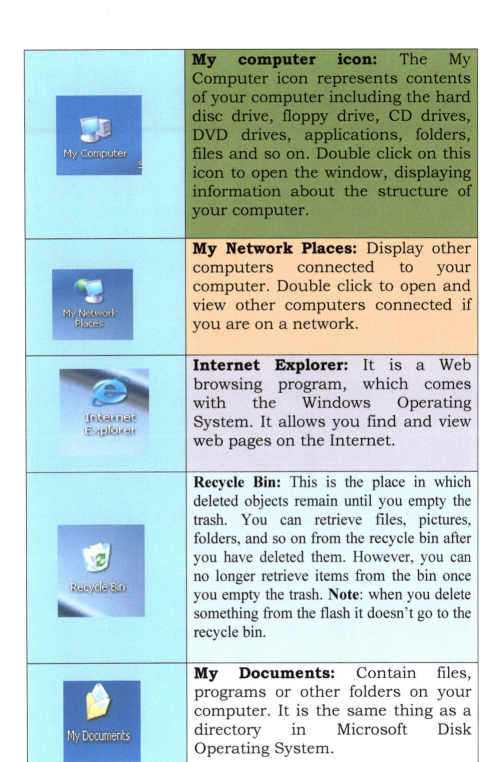 My Computer | **My computer icon:** The My Computer icon represents contents of your computer including the hard disc drive, floppy drive, CD drives, DVD drives, applications, folders, files and so on. Double click on this icon to open the window, displaying information about the structure of your computer. |
| My Network Places | **My Network Places:** Display other computers connected to your computer. Double click to open and view other computers connected if you are on a network. |
| Internet Explorer | **Internet Explorer:** It is a Web browsing program, which comes with the Windows Operating System. It allows you find and view web pages on the Internet. |
| Recycle Bin | **Recycle Bin:** This is the place in which deleted objects remain until you empty the trash. You can retrieve files, pictures, folders, and so on from the recycle bin after you have deleted them. However, you can no longer retrieve items from the bin once you empty the trash. **Note**: when you delete something from the flash it doesn't go to the recycle bin. |
| My Documents | **My Documents:** Contain files, programs or other folders on your computer. It is the same thing as a directory in Microsoft Disk Operating System. |

| 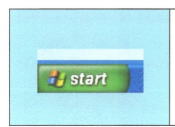 | **Start button:** This is very important as it is used to open up a **Start Menu,** which has various options including running programs and turning off your computer. |

## Using the Mouse

You use the mouse to perform many actions in windows and windows applications. With the mouse, you can easily select an icon, folder or window among other things.

## Selecting involves two steps:

## Pointing and Clicking.

You can move an item by clicking and dragging it. To click, point the mouse pointer at the object or item you want to select. When using the mouse, click the left mouse button unless the directions specify otherwise. The right mouse button can be used when you want to display a shortcut or a quick menu. The items on the menu depend on the object you are right-clicking. To double-click an item, you point to the item and press and release the left mouse button twice in quick succession.

**To drag an object to a new location on screen,** point to the object, press and hold down the left mouse button, move the mouse to a new location, and release the mouse button.

You also can perform certain actions, such as **selecting multiple actions or copying items** by performing two additional mouse operations (Shift + Click and Ctrl + Click).

**Click** – means to press the left mouse button. **Right-click** – means to press the right mouse button. **Double click** – means to press the left mouse button twice in quick succession. **Shift + Click** – means to press and hold down the Shift key and then click the left mouse button while pointing to various items. **Ctrl + Click** – is to press and hold down the Ctrl key, and then click the left mouse button. The result of either of these actions depends upon where you are in windows.

Mouse comes in different shapes, sizes and buttons. There are three categories of computer mouse: Three button mice have primary button, secondary button and a middle button between these two. Scroll mouse replaces the middle button of the three button mouse with a small roller. When roller is moved forward and backward, the screen moves in downward and upward direction. Cordless mouse are not physically connected with the computer. They rely on infrared or radio waves to communicate with the computer.

**Windows XP Start Button**

Provide access to many elements in windows e.g. Programs, documents and so on. The ones below are those displayed by your start menu and may display more depending on what is installed on your computer.

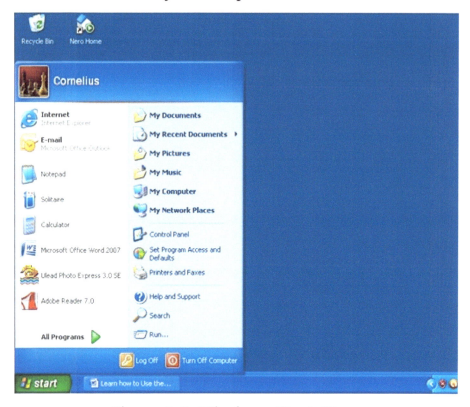

Figure 2.3: **Windows Start Menu**

**Turn off:** Displays the turn off computer dialog box in which you prepare your computer before turning it off.

**Log off:** Allows you to log off or on to windows so that another user can logon.

**Run:** Enables you to run a program from hard disc drive, floppy, CD or DVD disks.

**Help and Support:** Displays help and support for performing tasks and procedures in windows.

**Search:** Enables you to search for files, folders or computers.

50

**Printers and Faxes:** Display printers and faxes that are installed on your computer. It also contains the Add Printer wizard to add a new printer to your computer.

**Set Program Access and Defaults:** Displays a dialog box via which you can change or remove programs, add new programs, add remove windows components and set program access and defaults on your computer.

**Control Panel:** It is used for customizing your windows setup.

**My Recent Documents:** Displays up to 15 of the most recent documents for quick and easy access, click the document name and the application initializes.

**All Programs:** Displays a sub menu that includes windows accessory programs, online services, the internet explorer and other programs installed on your computer.

## Microsoft Windows 7 Start Button

**Start Menu**

In Windows 7, you have much more control over the programs and files that appear on the Start menu. The Start menu is essentially a blank slate that you can organize and customize to suit your preferences. Find a program you want to add and right click and choose add to start menu. Click on the Start button on left bottom corner. The Start menu list will appear and if you hold your mouse over the program you will see a list of recently opened files used by that program on the right.

51

This also shows the location the file was saved to.

**Shake**

Shake one window to make the others disappear. You can instantly snap your windows to size, and clear the desktop in one motion.

As widescreen monitors become more common, there is easier side-by-side window management and Windows 7 has it built in. The new Aero Shake feature lets you clear the desktop of all background windows by grabbing the top bar of the active window and

Figure 2.4: **Windows 7 Start Menu**

moving it back and forth quickly.

**Pin**

Pin your favorite programs right to your taskbar. Pinning programs to the taskbar complements pinning programs to the Start menu, like in earlier versions of Windows. When you pin a favorite program to the taskbar, you can always see it there and easily access it with a single click. Windows 7 also includes Jump Lists, so that in addition to launching a program from the taskbar, you can now launch favorite and recent items from that program, just by clicking the same button. You can also move these around to be in the order you want.

Figure 2.5: **Pinned programs to task bar windows 7**

**Jump Lists**

Jump Lists are lists of recently or frequently opened items, such as files, folders, tasks, or websites, organized by the program that you use to open them. In addition to being able to open recent items using a Jump List, you can also pin favorite items to a Jump List so you can quickly get to the items that you use every day.

On the taskbar, Jump Lists appear for programs that you have pinned to the taskbar and programs that are currently running. You can view the Jump Lists for a program by right-clicking the taskbar button, or by dragging the button toward the desktop. You open items from the Jump Lists by clicking on them.

**Snap**

Easily look at two windows side by side. Drag to one side it will snap into place. Drag back and it will go to its previous position. Maximize window by double clicking on the top bar. To snap two windows in windows 7, open two application programs, right click on an empty portion of the taskbar then choose Show windows side by side from the pop-up menu. You could also choose Undo show windows side by side from the pop-up menu to cause one window to maximize itself.

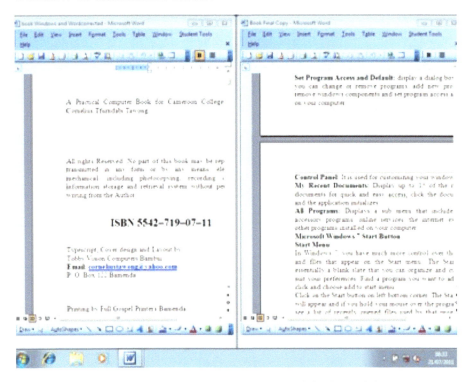

Figure 2.7: **Two windows side by side.**

**Windows Search**

Instantly find anything on your computer. Click on the Start button on left bottom corner.

Click into the **Search programs and files** area and start typing in the Search dialog box.

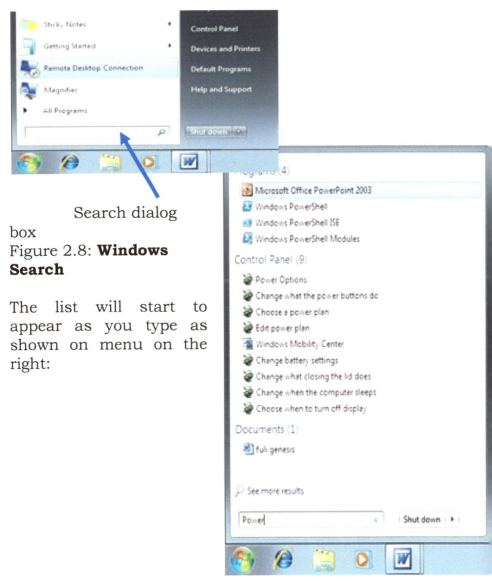

Search dialog box

Figure 2.8: **Windows Search**

The list will start to appear as you type as shown on menu on the right:

**Libraries**

Libraries are a new way to see your files in windows 7. Libraries are not folders but areas to locate and find your files. They do not store your files but gather the files in a way for you to easily locate them. So in other words, in the library are your files that are located in folders in various locations. The four Libraries are Documents, Music, Pictures and Videos. You can also add an external device to show up in the Libraries. Click on the **Library** Icon found on your taskbar. The library area will appear as shown below.

**Active Directory/Network Password Expiring Details**

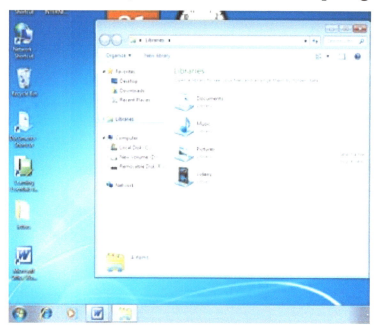

Figure 2.9: **Library area Windows 7**

The password prompt to change does not appear until approximately one week before it is about to expire. Press the **Ctrl + Alt + Delete** keys on your keyboard.

The Old Password and New Password and Confirm Password dialog boxes will need details to complete this password change.

## What is a library?

Libraries are new in Windows 7. Libraries are where you go to manage your documents, music, pictures, and other files. It is the location of your documents but more. You can browse your files the same way you would in a folder in Windows XP or you can view your files arranged by properties like date and type. In some ways, a library is similar to a folder. For example, when you open a library, you will see one or more files. However, unlike a folder, a library gathers files that are stored in several locations. This is a slight, but important difference. Libraries do not actually store your items. They monitor folders that contain your items, and let you access and arrange the items in different ways.

For instance, if you have music files in folders on your hard disk and on an external drive, you can access all of your music files at once using the Music library.

## How to create or change a library

Windows 7 has four default libraries:

## Documents, Music, Pictures, and Videos

You can also create new libraries.

-Right click on start button

-Click on open Windows Explorer, select Libraries

- Click on New Library, the new library icon appears

Type library name and validate. The new library appears in the libraries group. Here are some ways you can modify an existing library:

**Include or remove a folder.** Libraries gather content from included folders, or library locations. You can include up to fifty folders in one library.

**Change the default save location.** The default save location determines where an item is stored when it is copied, moved, or saved to the library.

**Change the type of file a library is optimized for.** Each library can be optimized for a certain file type (such as music or pictures). Optimizing a library for a certain file type changes the available options for arranging your files.

**What happens if you delete a library or the items in a library?** If you delete a library, the library itself is moved to the Recycle Bin. The files and folders that were accessible in the library are stored elsewhere and therefore are not deleted. If you accidentally delete one of the four default libraries (Documents, Music, Pictures, or Videos), you can restore it to its original state in the navigation pane by right-clicking **Libraries** and then clicking add.

**Restore default libraries**. If you delete files or folders from within a library, they are also deleted from their original locations. If you want to remove an item from a library but not delete it from the location it is stored in, you should remove the folder containing the item. When you remove a folder from a library, all the items in the folder will be removed (but not deleted).

## Preview Document in Folder

Once you find your file you can preview it right inside the folder without opening up the program. Select the file you want to Preview, and then click on the Preview Pane button.

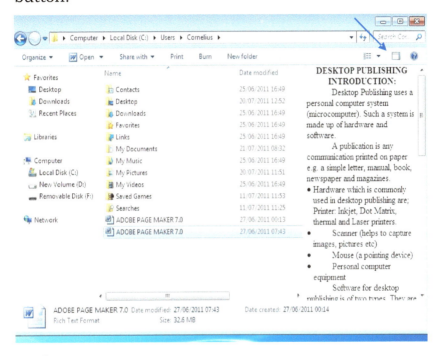

## Gadgets

Right click desktop and drag over to your desktop what gadgets you would like, the news, your pictures and the phases of the moon, right on your desktop. Here are some examples:

Figure 2.11 **Gadgets**

**Burn to a CD or Send as Email**

In Windows 7 you can write or burn a file to a blank CD or DVD. Select the files you want to burn and click on the **Burn** button found on the toolbar within the Library area. You can also send a document as an email attachment by clicking on **E-mail.**

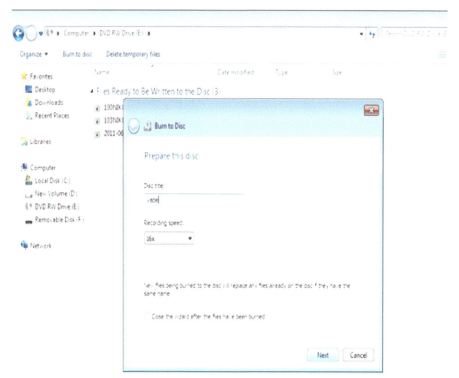

## Calculate more

At first glance the Windows 7 calculator basics, but you will see powerful new Statistics and Programmer views. Try the Options menu to find different unit conversions (length, weight, volume and more), date calculations (how many days between two dates), and spreadsheet–type templates to help you calculate vehicle mileage, mortgage rates and more.

## Problem Steps Recorder

If users have a problem with their computer, Windows 7 comes to the rescue with the in-built diagnostic tool called the Problem Steps Recorder which provides a simple screen capture tool. Problem Steps Recorder which enables you to record a series of actions. Once you hit **record**, it tracks your mouse and keyboard and captures screenshots with any comments you choose to associate alongside them. Once you stop recording, it saves the whole thing to a ZIP file, containing an HTML (hypertext makeup language) based **slide show** of the steps. It is a really an efficient little tool.

## The Snipping Tool

The Snipping Tool can capture a screen shot of anything on your desktop, like a paragraph in a document, a picture you are editing, or a section of a webpage. When you want to share an idea or ask a question, it is a great way to show a co-worker or fellow students what you are talking about. Instead of writing down the error message, just snip it.

Snip a whole window, a rectangular section of the screen, or draw a freehand outline with your mouse or tablet pen.

## Improved WordPad

WordPad in Windows 7 has undergone a major renovation. Think of it as a lite version of Microsoft Word. WordPad has a spiffy ribbon interface, making it a snap to create well-formatted documents. WordPad now supports the Office Open XML document (.DOCX) format. This makes it even easier to open .DOCX files created in Microsoft Word in WordPad.

## Help and Support

Click on the Start button, then on the Help and Support command to link for all kinds of helpful hints, tutorials and videos.

## Searching For Files in Windows 7

Start typing what you intend to search in the Search dialog box. Files and emails will appear as you type the words into the Search programs and files dialog box.

# Shut down Windows 7

Click on the Start button, then on Shut down. When you click **Shut down**, your computer closes all open programs and shuts down your computer.

**Windows 7 Shortcut Keys**

**On the shortcuts below the Win means holding down the Windows key on your keyboard**

**Win+Left Arrow**: Dock the current window to the left half of the screen

**Win+Right Arrow**: Dock the current window to the right half of the screen

**Win+Up Arrow**: Maximize the current window.

**Win+Down Arrow**: If the current window is maximized or minimized

**Win+Home**: Minimize all but the current window

**Win+F**:      Launch a Search Window

**Win+G**:      Cycle through Gadgets

**Win+Space**: Aero Peek the Desktop

**Win+Plus +**: Zoom Out

**Win+Minus -**: Zoom In

**Alt+F4**:      Close the active window

**Alt+Tab**:      Switch to previous active window

**Alt+Esc**:      Cycle through all open windows

**Win+Tab**:      Flip 3D

**Ctrl+Win+Tab**: Persistent Flip 3D

**Win+T**:      Cycle through applications on taskbar (showing its live preview)

**Win+M**:      Minimize all open windows

**Win+Shift+M**: Undo all window minimization

**Win+D**:      Toggle showing the desktop

**Win+L**:      Lock the desktop (Ctrl, Alt, Delete will prompt to log back in)

**Uses of the Taskbar**

It contains four items that act as shortcuts, thus eliminating the use of start menu to launch programs or to create shortcuts on your desktop. It also displays buttons representing open windows and applications. You can quickly switch through windows by clicking the button on the taskbar.

You can move the taskbar to the right, top or left side of the screen to customize your work space. To do this, click the mouse anywhere on the bar – except on a button – drag the taskbar to your desired location of the screen. As you drag, it relocates to the area. You can easily drag it to the bottom if you prefer it there. **Note**: If you cannot display the task bar, press the Windows key or press Ctrl+Esc to display and open start menu. From start button, settings and taskbar you can hide or restore the taskbar by putting a check mark or not on the auto hide box check box.

**Quitting Windows XP**

Click on Start button

Click on Turn off Computer

Turn off Computer dialog box appears

Click Turn off

Figure 2.13 **Turn off computer dialog box**

**Note:** Before you turn off your computer, always turn off windows by clicking start button and choosing Turn Off. This results in a safe turn off and helps prevent files from being corrupted and is known as soft turn off.

**Working with a Window**

When you start up a program, it appears on the desktop in a Window, and a button also appears on the taskbar representing that program. You can use these buttons to switch between programs by clicking on them with the mouse. When the program is closed, the button disappears.

A Window is a box area in which you view programs, files, folders, drives, icons representing programs, files or folders and other elements.

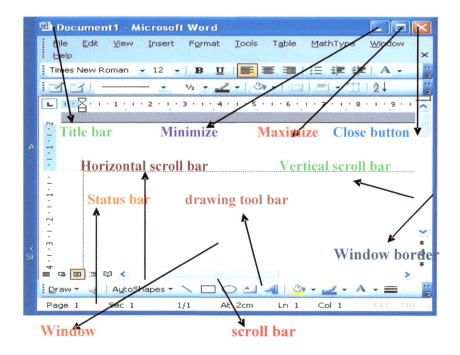

Many of the components are the same for all windows in windows XP, Windows 7 and windows applications which makes it easy for you to manage your work.

## Window Elements

| Element | Description |
|---|---|
| Title bar | Contains the window's name, the control menu, and close buttons |
| Menu bar | Contains menus with related commands and options that help you control window and its contents |
| Control menu buttons | Use in place of minimize, maximize, restore and close buttons. Can also be used to size and move a window. |

| Toolbars | Display graphic tool buttons that represent shortcuts to various menu commands |
|---|---|
| Minimize button | Reduces window to a button on the taskbar |
| Maximize button | Enlarges the window to full screen |
| Close button | Closes the window and if a program is running in the window, exits the program |
| Folders | Icons within windows that represent directories; folders and files. |
| Files | Icons representing documents-spreadsheet, databases, program files, and other files stored in folders on a drive or floppy disk. |
| Window border | A rim around the window use to resize the window |
| Status bar | A bar across the bottom of the window that describes the contents of the window |
| Scroll bar | Vertical or horizontal bar that enables you to move the internal viewing area of a window. |
| Menu | Shows headings for menus that will appear if heading is clicked. A typical menu (File) is shown here: it options |

| | include Open, Save, Exit etc. |
|---|---|

## Sizing a window

You may want to increase the size of a window to see it full contents, or you may want to decrease a window to a button on the taskbar to make room for other windows. One of the ways is to use maximize, minimize, or restore commands found on the control menu. If you use the mouse, you will use maximize, minimize and restore buttons located at the right end of the window's title bar.

**Note:** When a window is maximize the restore button replaces the maximize button.

At some point you will need to size the window's border to suit your needs. You might want to fit two or more windows on screen at the same time. Note – a window's border appears only on a restored window, not on a maximized or minimized window. To size a window border, follow these steps:

- Place mouse pointer on the portion of the border that you want to resize. When the mouse is positioned correctly, it changes shape to a double–headed arrow. Use the double headed arrow to resize the window as required.

**Scroll bar –** Is a bar that contains three items: two scroll arrows and a scroll box. You use the scroll arrows and a scroll box to move around in the window, scrolling a line at a time, or even a page at a time because all of the hard disc drive window's contents are not fully visible.

**Moving a window** – Is as important as resizing one. To do this, point at the window's title bar, press and hold the left mouse button, and drag the window to its new location.

**Default** – Is the initial settings of a program. In other words, how a program will look and respond without intervention on your part. Program defaults can be changed e.g. in Microsoft Word you can change the default font scheme.

**Closing a Window**

- Click close button on title bar
- Choose File, Close

    Or

- ➢ Press Alt + F4

**To quickly close several windows** that are open in Microsoft Word 2003 Window, hold the Shift key while clicking close button on the last window you opened.

**Note**: Closing windows in applications will close a file or document keeping the program opened but all other key strokes described will close the actual application.

**Menus**

A menu is a list of commands that you use to perform tasks in windows and windows applications (tasks such as deleting and copying selected items). They are organized in logical groups and are context sensitive i.e. different menu options and different menus themselves will appear within the menu depending on the task you are currently performing e.g. if you haven't cut or copy text, the paste command on the Edit menu is not available (it is *grayed out*). You find menus on the menu bar and can also get them when you right-click an item the later known as pop-up menus.

Items on the menu bar are organized to help you find the command you want. Items related to editing are grouped together whereas those to arranging, opening files and so on.

**Tool bar buttons** – They represent common commands such as cut, copy, undo, and so on. Tools available depend on window or application you are using.

**Pull down menu** – A menu that appears to pull down from the menu bar. You access the menu by clicking its name in the menu bar. When you will become familiar with windows and our various windows applications, you will need to use the menus to view and select commands. However, after you have worked in windows for a while you will probably want to use shortcut keys for commands you use often. They enable you to select commands without using the menus. Generally, shortcut keys combine the Alt, Ctrl, or Shift key with a letter key such as S. If a shortcut is available; it is listed on the pull down menu to the right of the command.

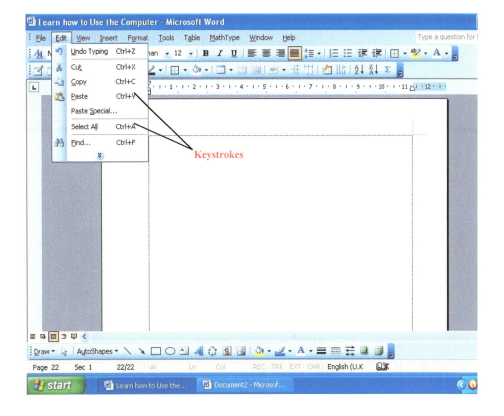

Figure 2.15 **Pull down menu showing shortcuts**

## Using Dialog Boxes

Windows and windows applications use dialog boxes to exchange information with you. A dialog box asks for related information the program needs in order to complete the operation. They vary in complexity depending on the program, the procedure and the number of options, in the actual box. Thus if you want to save a new file, you will be asked to supply a filename and to indicate the drive and directory/folder where the file will be located. To make these requests, Windows applications use a dialog box.

71

The following list briefly explains the components of a dialog box.

**1.) Textbox** – Provides a place to type an entry, such as filename, path, font, or measurement.

**2.) List box** – Presents a line up (slate) of possible options from which you can choose. Scroll bars often accompany a list box so you can view items on the list.

**3.) Drop down list box** – This is a single line list box with a drop down arrow button to the right of it. Click the arrow for a drop down display of choices.

**4.) Option button** – Present a group of related choices from which you can choose one. Click the option button you want to select and all others become deselected.

**5.) Check box** – Enables you to turn an option off or on. A check mark appears in the box next to any option that is active (turned on).

**6.) Command button** – When selected, carries out the command displayed on the button (Open, Ok, Help, Cancel, Quit).

**7.) Tabs** – Represent multiple sections of a dialog box. Only one tab is displayed at a time and each tab contains related options.

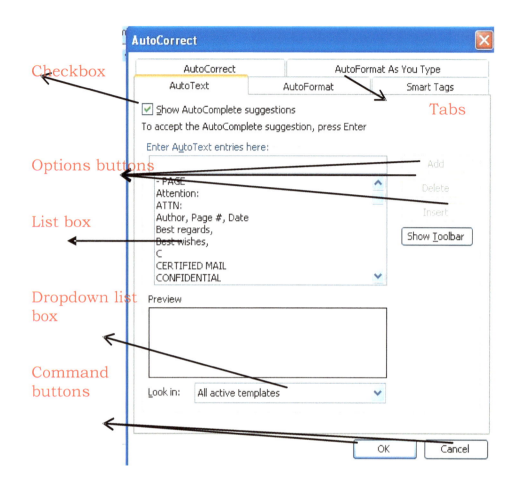

Figure 2.16 **The Auto Correct Dialog Box**

# The Autocorrect Dialog Box in Microsoft Word 2003

## Editing Keys for Textboxes and other Text

| Key | Description |
| --- | --- |
| Delete | Deletes the character to the right of the insertion point |
| Back space | Deletes the character to the left of the insertion point |
| End | Moves the insertion point to the end of line |
| Home | Moves insertion point to the beginning of line |
| Arrow keys | Moves insertion point one character in the direction of the arrow |
| Shift + End | Selects the text from insertion point to end of line |
| Shift + Home | Selects the text from insertion point to beginning of line |
| Shift + Arrow key | Selects the next character in the direction of the arrow |
| Ctrl + C | Copy selected text to clipboard |
| Ctrl + X | Cut selected text to clipboard |
| Ctrl + V | Pastes the selected text from clipboard |

* **Clipboard** – is a provision by windows that holds any cut or copied text for you so you can paste to another location.

**Working with Files, Folders and Disks**

When you install windows based software, the installation program creates a folder for the programs to reside in on your hard disc drive. "Microsoft Office" for example, is automatically placed in a folder called "Program Files". This is done to keep the software separate from other programs you may have loaded or installed on your computer.

When you create a document; spreadsheet, database, or any other file, you determine where it will reside on your hard drive when you save it. If you have Microsoft Office 2003, Microsoft Office 2007, Microsoft Office 2010, Microsoft Office 2013 etc installed office creates a default folder called "My documents". When you save a document using one of the windows products, such as Microsoft Word or Microsoft Excel, those documents will be saved in "My documents" folder unless you instruct the program otherwise.

**Managing Files and Folders**

There are two common ways of managing files using Windows. The first way is to use **My Computer icon**, which you can access by clicking the My Computer icon on the Desktop. The second way is to use **Windows Explorer** (by right-clicking i.e. click the **Start** button with the **right mouse button** and then choosing **Explore**). These programs enable you to carry out many basic housekeeping operations with your files. You can create folders, move files, copy, rename or delete them, format discs, and many other essential operations.

## Creating a Folder

Right click on **start button**

Click on **Explore**

Select drive on which you want the folder to be placed

Click on File menu

Select New,

Folder, and the New Folder icon appears

Type folder name and validate by clicking out of the folder. Windows allows you to use up to 255 characters, including spaces, for your folder's name. You may not use any of the following characters which have special meaning to the operating system. \ / : * ? < > |. Windows usually warns you that you cannot use these characters if you accidentally include one in your folder name.

To quickly see files, folders and drives and how files and folders are organized, click the My Computer icon on desktop. Some of the icons in the My Computer icon window represent drives; in this case, A: represents floppy drive, C: the computer's hard disk drive, D: The CD Rom drive. Your drive letters might be assigned different depending on the number of drives installed on your computer.

## Getting a screen dump

Some times you may want to **capture** an image from the Windows screen, i.e. save as a graphic image, which can be inserted into other documents. You capture the image (known as a **screen dump),** by pressing the **Print**

**Screen** key on your keyboard. The image will be stored in the clipboard. If you want to edit a screen dump, paste it into Paint or another graphics application. You can then make changes to it, and save it as a file which can be inserted into a word processed document or other file.

**The My Computer Window**

The menu bar on my computer window offers six choices. File, Edit, View, Favorite, Tools and Help.

The File menu contains commands pertaining to file management, such as creating new folders, creating shortcuts, deleting or renaming files or folders, checking files or folder properties, and closing the window.

The Edit menu contains editing functions. Here the undo command will undo your last action. Use cut to remove a file or folder and store it in the clipboard and paste to put the contents of the clipboard in a selected window. Choose Select All to select all of the files and folders in the window. Select All is useful when you are deleting, copying or moving several files at one time. Under View Menu are a series of options for viewing files and folders with differently sized icons or in different order. Favorite menu contains commands you can add and organise your favorites and Tools menu contains commands to help you map a network drive, disconnect a network drive and synchronize your homepage.

**Help systems.** Help about general usage of the computer and how to use the features of Windows is built into the computer, and it is available by clicking the **Start** button and choosing **Help and Support.**

**Selecting Files and Folders**

Before you perform an operation on a file or folder, you must select (or highlight) the item so windows know which one you want to use.

To select files or folders:

**Single file or folder** – Point to the file or folder, or use the arrow keys to move the highlighting to the file or folder icon you want to select.

**Multiple continuous files or folders:** Point to the first file or folder icon, hold down Shift key, and point to last file or folder icon. You can also use Shift and arrow key.

**Multiple non–continuous files** – Point to first file, hold down Ctrl key, and point to each of additional files you want.

All file or folder icons in the window. Choose Edit, Select All from the menu or press Ctrl + A

**Note:** After you have selected your files, hold down the Ctrl key and point at the files (one at a time) that you do not wish to include in your selection.

## Moving Files and Folders

Done by copying and pasting or by using your mouse to drag and drop in a new location. **Note:** When you delete a file, text or an item in windows you are either deleting it permanently or sending it to the Recycle bin, depending on your windows default settings. Items that you cut are sent to the windows clipboard and remained there until you replace the clipboard contents with something new.

When using the cut and paste method, be careful not to copy or cut another item before you paste your items in its new location, as the new item you cut or copy will replace the item you already had stored in the clipboard.

**Copy and Paste –** Skills you can use in other windows programs such as Microsoft Works, Microsoft Excel and other programs that are not Microsoft but designed to run under windows.

**Copying to the Flash Memory** – Click the selected icons with right mouse button and choose Send To, Choose Removable disk (E) from popup menu.

## Deleting Files and Folders

When deleted, they are removed from current window and placed in the Recycle bin. If necessary can be recovered if trash is not emptied. However if the file is on a flash memory it doesn't go to the Recycle Bin. So be very sure you want to delete files from a flash memory.

**Renaming Files and Folders**

Right click mouse button on Folder Fr. Joachim as shown below. Choose Rename from popup or context sensitive menu. Type a new name for the folder and click outside the folder to validate.

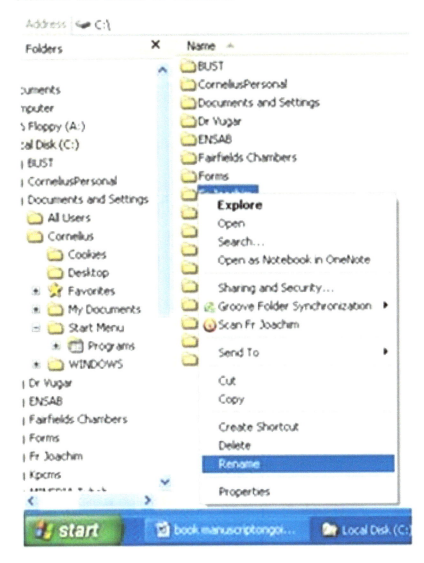

Figure 2.17 **Renaming Folders**

**Shortcuts**

They provide easy access to files and programs. A quick method is to use the right mouse button to send it to the desktop. It is also possible to create shortcuts directly from start menu. Some shortcuts are created when you install programs. To remove unwanted shortcuts from the desktop, drag them over to the Recycle bin and release the mouse button when the Recycle bin is highlighted.

**Searching Files Windows XP Users**

When you are not sure of a file name or the folder where it is stored, My Computer has a Search feature to help you search for the file.

➢ Open My Computer window

➢ Select drive you want to search, such as C:

- ➢ Select folder
- ➢ Choose File, Search from the menu.
- ➢ The Search Results dialog box appears
- ➢ Enter name of file you want to search

**Note:** If you don't know the complete name use an asterisk (*) to substitute the beginning or end of name (such as **\*ine** to search all files that end in **ine);** use a question sign (?) to substitute for a character you don't know. Choose Options, case sensitive from menu if you want to find or search a file that is in uppercase but not find a file with the same name that is in lowercase. The 'Look in' box should show name of drive you selected. Click include subfolders to search through all folders in specified drive.

Use browse to select a folder or network drive

Click Search.

When the search is complete, a list of files or folders matching your search criteria appears at the bottom of the dialog box.

When you store or save files, use naming conventions that you will remember and understand later, particularly when you will need find a file e.g. name files you need for your job information with word job followed by a date (8 – 01 – 2013) or account number. Next January when you are looking for all your job records you can search for job*2013*.

**Windows Explorer**

Unlike My Computer, the Windows Explorer does not show you the contents of just one folder at one time. Instead everything is contained within one window. The list of all the drives and folders on your system or network is on the left pane, and the contents of the selected folder or drive on the right pane. This arrangement makes it easier to navigate when you need to look at different drives and folders.

**To open the Windows Explorer:**

1.) Right click on the Start button

1.) Select Explore from pop-up menu

2.) The Start menu Window appears

The right pane displays the contents of the selected drive or folder. The folders pane which normally appears on the left side of the Explorer Window has icons representing drives.

**Note:** Your drive letter designation could be different. If you have a Zip drive, tape drive, external hard drive or an additional floppy drive, icons for those items will also appear in this window. The hard drive by default is C:\drive while the floppy drive is designated A:\drive. If your hard drive is partitioned or if you have additional drives, the letters D:\, E:\, F:\ and so on are assigned. The flash is usually the removable drive. You will see icons for the Recycle bin, My Network places, and Shared documents if you are using Windows XP.

The remaining icons in the Folders pane look like manila folder icons. When you create documents with an application such as a word processor, you save them as files. In order not to have the files haphazardly scattered across your hard disc drive (HDD), you store them in folders.

Your program files are also stored in a folder "Program Files". Some folders contain other folders.

The Folders pane shows you the hierarchy of drives and folders. Here you can see clearly which folders reside inside other folders because the inside folders (called "subfolders") are indented under the main folder and are tied to the main folder by a line. In front of some of the folders or drive icons in the Folders pane you will see (+) or (–) signs.

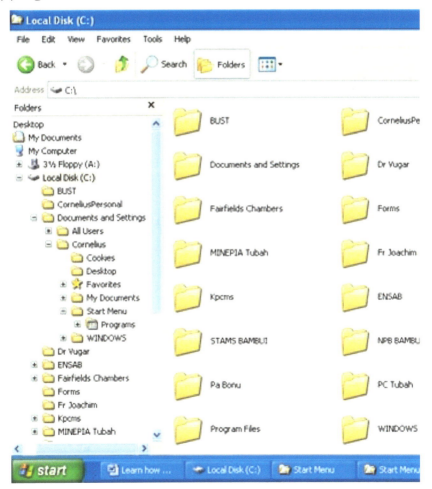

Figure 2.18 **Showing Folders Pane Windows Explorer**

85

(+) means the folder or drive has folders inside but you cannot see the list at the moment because it is collapsed. Click the (+) sign in the Folders pane to expand it, and then you will see the folders listed below.

 (–) appears in front of drive or folder icon.

To collapse the folder or drive so you no longer see the folders under it, click the (–) sign.

**Note** the change from   (–) to (▣) and (–) to (▢) in Windows 7 respectively.

To see the full contents of a drive or folder click it. The folder opens up. The folder and files that the selected drive contains appears in the contents pane. These files have different icons depending on what type of file they are or what program they represent or were created in. If you need more room in either pane point to the dividing border between the panes until the mouse pointer becomes a two–headed arrow, and then drag left or right to increase the size of left or right pane.


**Using File Viewing Options**

Not all files are displayed when you open a folder. Some system files are hidden. Also, if you are accustomed to DOS (Disk Operating System), you probably noticed that no file extensions appear in windows.


**Folder Options Overview**

With Folder Options, you can specify how your folders function and how content is displayed.

For example, you can indicate that you want your folders to display hyperlinks to common tasks, other storage locations, and detailed file information. You can also choose to open items with either a single or a double click.

You can change the **program** that opens a file type. You can also change the items that appear on your **desktop.**

To change folder options settings, open Folder Options in Control Panel. Or, to open Folder Options from a folder window, click **Tools Menu**, and then click **Folder Options**.

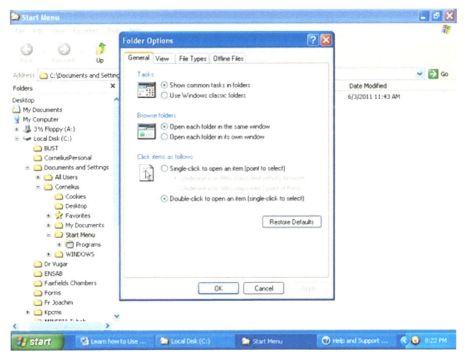

Figure 2.19 **Folder Options**

**File Properties**

All storage media (hard disk, flash memory, DVDs, CDs) measure their capacity in bytes. A byte is approximately the size of one character roughly a thousand bytes is a kilobyte (1024 bytes = 1 kilobyte), abbreviated KB, a million bytes is a megabyte (abbreviated MB, called "meg") and a billion bytes is a gigabyte (abbreviated GB, called "gig").

File sizes are measured in bytes. That does not mean that a one thousand (1.000) character essay equals one thousand (1.000) bytes. All the formatting directions in a document also take up space.

If you know the size of files you want to store and you know the storage capacity of the disk you want to store them on, you can tell if the disk is large enough to hold the files. It is the free space of the disk that must be large enough to hold your files. When you select a drive in **My Computer** or **Windows Explorer**, the capacity of the drive and the amount of free space appears on the status bar and on the left side of My Computer window.

**File Creation Date and Time:** When you first save a file, windows automatically records the date and time that you saved it. When you open the file and make changes, the date and time you save it are again recorded as the modified date.

Back up programs use this information to determine which files have been modified since the last backup. Also, if you know the date you last modified a file but cannot remember the name, you can search for it by date.

The date and time are dependent upon the system clock, so be sure to set yours for the correct time (by selecting Date, Time, Language, and Regional Options icon in Control Panel).

## File Attributes

There are four attributes that can be assigned to files:

## Read only

You can open a read–only file and read it or print it, but you cannot change it or delete it. This protects the original file from being changed.

## Hidden

Some files are not visible in file listings, and you can't use them unless you know the name of the file. Program files may be hidden to keep you from deleting them accidentally.

## Archive

Some programs use this option to determine which files are to be backed up. In most cases, if the file is not read–only it has an archive attribute.

## System

Certain files are necessary to the operation of your computer; these are system files.

**Note**: When you open My Computer or Windows Explorer in Detail View, you can see which files are system files under the Attributes Column, if you enabled that option in Folder Options Overview e.g. the file in the window below named kpcms having file size 1KB and file type configuration settings with date modified 4/11/2001 at 1:02pm is a system file.

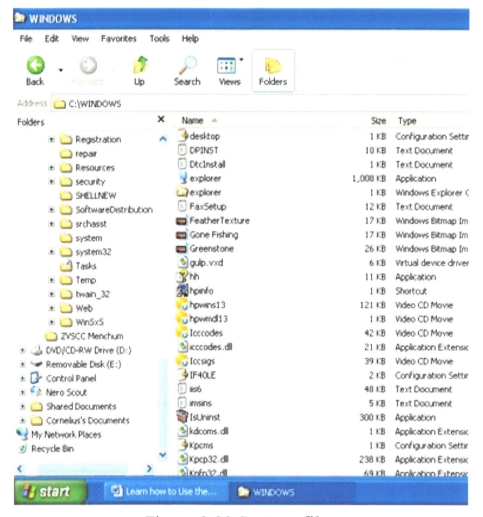

Figure 2.20 **System files**

## Viewing Properties

To see the properties of a file – whether in My Computer, Windows Explorer, My Network Places – you must first select the file and then do one of the following:

- ❖ Click on File Menu, then select Properties
- ❖ The Properties dialog box appears

Figure 2.21 File **Properties dialog box**

The properties dialog box provides you with information about the file: Type of file, Opening program, Location, Size in kilobytes, Size on disk, When created, When modified, Accessed, Attributes (Read only, Archive, hidden, system)

Except for system files, you can change the attributes of selected files by checking the attributes you want to assign them. For example if you want to provide a file to several users for reference but you do not want them to change the file, change the file attribute to read-only.

Click Apply to change an attribute without closing the Properties dialog box; click Ok to accept the changes.

## Working with Flash Memories

### Formatting flash memories

One way to store your files or take them along with you is to copy them onto flask memories or external hard drives. Reliable pre-formatted disks are available for little more than the price of unformatted disks, so the need to format your flask memories is not as prevalent as it once was with floppy disks. However, you may prefer to format your own or want to format a previously used flask memory to thoroughly erase it and start afresh.

Formatting divides a disk into tracks and sectors so that the Operating System can find and identify the files stored on the disk.

Formatting erases all of the files on a disk, so be sure to check the disk contents thoroughly before you format it.

### To format a flash memory

Open My Computer or the Windows Explorer.

Close all other windows that display information about or are using the drive you are about to format. Select the flash memory (usually Removable drive (E:, F:, G:,...) Right click on it, click on Format

The Format Removable Disk (E:) dialog box appears.

Select Format type

Quick Format removes all the files from the disk without scanning for bad sectors. Use this only on disks that have been previously formatted.

To give a name to the disk that helps identify it, type a name in the Volume label box. You can use up to eleven characters.

Click Start button on the format dialog box.

The result of formatting appears when process is complete. Click close to close the dialog box.

**Copying disks** – Means making an exact duplicate of the original disk including hidden, compressed and Figure 2.22

**Format dialog box**

system files.

In Microsoft Disk Operating System (MS DOS) this method is the same as using the Disk copy command.

**Naming Disks** – Many people don't apply labels to their disks because they frequently change the contents. They prefer to rely on the marker label on the outside of the disk.

**Importing Pictures and Videos from a Digital Camera**

Connect the camera to a USB port or remove the camera memory and slot into a memory card reader.

Connect your card reader to the Universal Serial Bus (USB) port. A prompt will indicate on screen. Click on import Pictures and Videos, the import picture and videos AutoPlay dialog box appears.

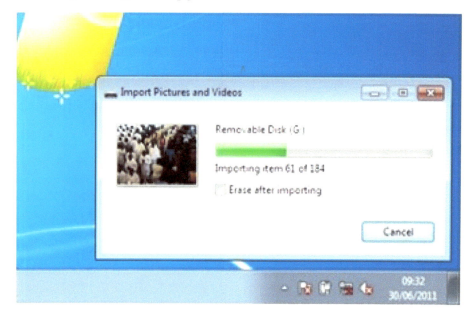

Figure 2.23 **Importing Pictures and Videos**

When the import Pictures and Videos AutoPlay dialog box process completes, your pictures are automatically downloaded to your computer and stored on the imported pictures and videos folder in the Picture library as shown below. You can now double click on a picture and use any picture editing software to view and edit your picture.

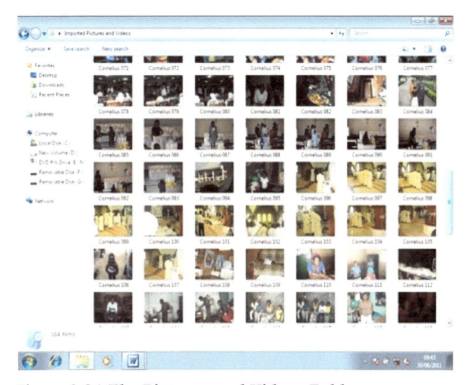

Figure 2.24 **The Pictures and Videos Folder**

95

## USING MICROSOFT PAINT

**What is Paint?** It is a Windows graphic program that allows you to create drawings you can use, either alone or in other windows application such as Microsoft Word, Lotus Word Pro or Corel Word Perfect.

### Starting Paint

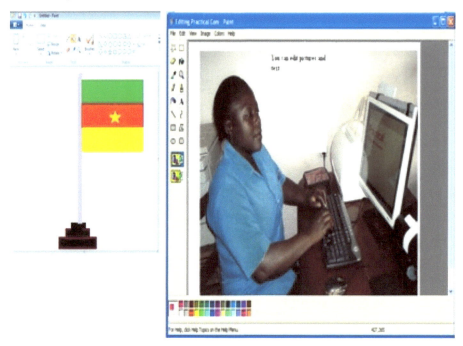

Figure2.25.i.ii. **Paint Windows**

- Click on Start button ( **Start** )

- Click on All Programs

- Point to Accessories

- Click on Paint

- The Paint Window initializes

### Outline and Fill colours

The overlapping boxes to the left of the colours palette in the Paint window show the currently selected

96

outline colour (the box on top and to the left) and the fill (the box underneath and to the right). The outline colour is the colour you use when you draw lines and outlines for objects, and the fill colour is the colour of the inside of any object you draw.

The box below the toolbar identifies the width of a line and the options for the currently selected tool in the tool box. Depending on which tool is selected, you use this box to determine how wide a line the line tool draws, how wide the eraser is, whether a shape is filled or transparent, etc.

Paint in Microsoft Windows 7 has been updated for you to have more shapes.

**Drawing in Paint**

Drawing with a mouse can be difficult at first, but practice always makes a difference. You use your mouse to draw lines, curves, and shapes as well as to enter text in Paint. The following list describes different ways to draw:

❖ To select the fill colour, right click any colour in the fill palette.

❖ To select line colour, click any colour in the palette.

❖ To select size of drawing, choose Image, Attributes and enter the width and height in the attributes dialog box then click Ok.

❖ The new size is defined by eight small black handles or boxes, outlining the specified area.

❖ To choose the type of object you are going to draw, click a drawing tool in the tool box at the left of the Paint window. Try starting with either the rectangle tool, the ellipse tool, or the straight line tool to experiment before other tools as you learn more about the program.

**Note:** Choose size of drawing before beginning.

❖ To select a line width for any line, curve, rectangle, ellipse, etc,

Click the line size you want in the line box in the lower left corner of the Paint window.

❖ To draw an object, point at the area where you want the object to appear (within the box image area), press and hold down the left mouse button, drag mouse pointer until the object is the size you want.

**Skills Transfer**

**A Perfect Circle Every time:** Select the ellipse tool, hold down Shift key, and click and drag the mouse pointer. You can also use this technique to draw a perfect square with a rectangle tool or perfectly straight lines with the line tool.

❖ Method applies to many windows drawing, graphics, and word processing    programs.

**Adding Text to a Graphic**

Using the text tool, you can add text to a graphic such as a logo or illustration. To do this,

- ➢ Select text tool
- ➢ Drag the text tool to create a rectangle in which you will type the text.

A rectangle that will hold the text and an insertion point appear.

- ➢ Before you type, Choose View menu, Text Tool bar. The font's toolbar appears, so choose the font, size and attributes from the fonts toolbar.
- ➢ Click the insertion point within the rectangle and type your text, pressing Enter at the end of each line.

**Note:** Use select tool to move text or graphics

**Microsoft Paint Tools Palette**

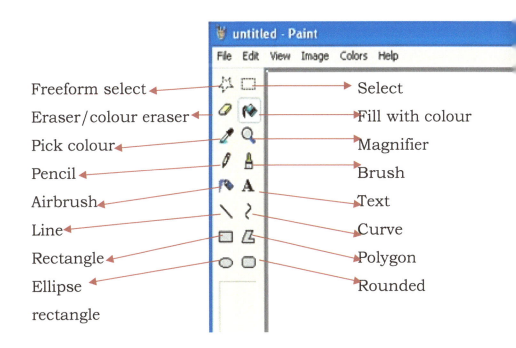

Figure 2.26: **Microsoft Paint The Tools Palette**

**Eraser tool:** It is used to erase colours, text or even images.

**Fill tool:** It is used to fill objects and work area with desired colour.

**Pencil tool:** It is used to draw free hand lines.

**Brush tool:** It is used to paint images with chosen colour.

**Airbrush:** It gives the spraying effect to the selected images with chosen colour. Whenever you use this tool on a desired image, a spray of dots appears over the image.

**Text tool:** It is used to type text in Paint window in different types of font.

**Ellipse tool:** It is used to draw circular shapes.

**Review Questions**

**How would you:**

- Use the My Music Folder?
- Open Windows Media Player?
- Play CDs?
- Play DVDs?
- Use the Media Guide?
- Copy Music from a CD?
- Use the Media Library?
- Create Playlists?
- Check for Player Updates?
- Use the Scanner and Camera Wizard?
- Use the My Pictures Folder?
- View Pictures with the Windows Picture and Fax Viewer?
- Listen to Internet Radio Stations?
- Copy Music to a CD or Device?
- Switch between Player Modes?
- Select Different Skins?
- View Visualizations?
- Change Visualizations?
- Modify Audio, Video, and Effects?
- Graphic Equalizer Video?
- Import Audio and Video?
- Create a New Collection?
- Create a Project?
- Create a New Project?
- Preview a Project?
- Save a Project?

- Edit a Digital Photo?
- Views?
- Rename a Digital Photo?
- Copy a Digital Photo?
- Move a Digital Photo?
- Delete a Digital Photo?
- View Photos as a Slide Show?
- Set a Slide Show as your Screen Saver?
- E-mail Digital Photos? Pinball?
- Use the Photo Printing Wizard?
- Order Prints Online? Backgammon?
- Open Windows Movie Maker? Checkers?
- Use the My Videos Folder?
- Get to Know the Windows Reversi?
- Movie Maker Environment? Spades?
- Record Audio and Video?

- Switch Workspace
- Zoom the Timeline?
- Record a Narration?
- Trim a Clip?
- Create a Transition?
- Delete a Clip?
- Save a Movie?
- Send a Movie?
- Play Space Cadet
- Play Spider Solitaire?
- Play Internet
- Play Internet
- Play Internet Hearts?
- Play Internet
- Play Internet

## Questions Microsoft Windows

Objective: Answer the following questions within the Microsoft Windows software. First, Open a Notepad Document.

Then, for each question write a brief description (1 or 2 sentences) explaining how you answered the question.

Answer Questions 1-8 pertaining to the same task

1. On the desktop, select the **Start Menu**. (E)

2. In the **Start Menu** select **Accessories**. (E)

3. Open **Notepad**. (E)

4. **Minimize** the Notepad window. (E)

5. Bring the Notepad window back up so that it is visible. (E)

6. **Maximize** the Notepad window. (E)

7. **Restore** the Notepad window. (E)

8. **Close** the Notepad window. (E)

**Answer Questions 9-18 pertaining to the same task**

9. On the desktop, open the **Recycle Bin** icon. (E)

10. **Arrange Icons** by **Name**. (M)

11. **Arrange Icons** by **Origin**. (M)

12. **Arrange Icons** by **Delete date**. (M)

13. **Arrange Icons** by **Type**. (M)

14. **Arrange Icons** by **Size**. (M)

15. **Select All Files** in the folder. (M)

16. Invert this selection. (M)

17. **Empty** the Recycle Bin. (M)

18. **Close** the Recycle Bin window. (E)

**Answer Questions 19-23 pertaining to the same task**

19. On the **Desktop** open **My Computer, Recycle Bin,** and **My Documents** (E)

20. Use the **Mouse** to choose **Recycle Bin** on the **Taskbar** (E)

21. Use the **Keyboard** to choose **My computer** on the **Taskbar** (D)

22. **Resize** the **My Computer** window (E)

23. **Close** all three windows (E)

**Answer Questions 24-38 pertaining to the same task**

24. On the desktop, use the **Start Menu** to **Explore** (D)

25. Highlight the **Desktop**. (E)

26. In the right pane, open **My Computer**, then open **(C:)**. (E)

27. In the right pane, open the **Program Files** folder. (E)

28. Click the **Up One Level** button. (D)

29. In the left pane, hide all subfolders. (M)

30. In the left pane, show all subfolders. (M)

31. Select **Search**. (M)

32. **Look In** "(C:)." (M)

33. In the "Named" box, enter "Windows." (M)

34. Perform the **search**. (E)

35. Scroll down the list of results. (E)

36. **Close** the Windows Explorer window. (E)

37. **Shut Down** the computer. (E)

38. Manually turn off the **Monitor**. (E)

**Answer Questions 39-57 pertaining to the same task**

39. **Create** a new folder on the desktop and call it "Ngwang's Folder." (M)

40. **Rename** the folder "Agbor's Folder." (M)

41. **Open** Agbor's Folder. (M)

42. Inside Agbor's Folder, **Create** a folder called "Lab Results." (D)

43. Inside Agbor's Folder, **Create** another folder called "Test Results." (D)

44. **Copy** the test Results folder. (M)

45. **Paste** the copy of the Test Results folder inside Agbor's Folder(M)

46. **Delete** the copy of the Test Results folder. (M)

47. Move the Lab Results folder inside the Test Results folder. (D)

48. **Cut** the Lab Results Folder. (D)

49. **Paste** the Lab Results folder back inside Agbor's Folder. (D)

50. Insert a Flash disk into your computer's USB port (E)

51. **Label** the Flash disk Sally (D)

52. **Format** Agbor's Disk (D)

53. Send Agbor's Folder to the Flash disk. (D)

54. **Delete** Agbor's Folder from the **Flash disk**. (D)

55. **Delete** Agbor's Folder from the **desktop**. (M)

56. **Write Protect** Agbor's Flash disk (D)

57. **Write Enable** Agbor's Flash disk (D)

**Answer Questions 58-67 pertaining to the same task**

58. In the **Start Menu**, click on **Help and Support**. (E)

59. Select the **Index Tab**. (M)

60. Perform a **Search** for "monitors". (M)

61. Select "troubleshooter." (D)

62. Scroll through the Windows XP Troubleshooter (M)

63. Use the **Search** to find information on printing (D)

64. Bookmark this topic as a **Favorite** (D)

65. Return to the **Contents** Section of **Help and Support** (M)

66. Locate printing quickly through **Favorites** (D)

67. **Close** the Help window. (E)

**Answer Questions 68-84 pertaining to the same task**

68. On the desktop, open the **My Computer** icon. (E)

69. Open the **Control Panel** icon. (M)

70. Open the **Day/Time** icon. (M)

71. Change the month to "December." (M)

72. Change the year to "2014." (M)

73. Change the time to "12:38PM." (M)

74. Change the time zone to "Mexico City." (D)

75. Cancel these changes. (E)

76. Open the **Fonts** icon. (E)

77. Insert the **Toolbar** (D)

78. Hide the **Toolbar**. (D)

79. View the files as **Large Icons**. (M)

80. View the files as a **List**. (M)

81. **List Fonts by Similarity**. (D)

82. **Select All** the fonts. (M)

83. **Invert** your selection. (M)

84. **Close** the Fonts window. (E)

**Answer Questions 85-91 pertaining to the same task**

85. Open the **Multimedia** icon (E)

86. In the **Audio Tab**, move all Playback Volumes to their highest setting (D)

87. Move each Recording Volume to its lowest setting (D)

88. Change the Recording Quality to **Telephone Quality** (D)

89. In the **Video Tab**, show video in **Full Screen** (D)

90. In the **MIDI Tab**, change the MIDI Output to **Custom Configuration** (D)

91. Cancel these changes (E)

**Answer Questions 92-100 pertaining to the same task**

92. Open the **Display** menu (D)

93. Change the **Wallpaper** on the desktop to clouds (D)

94. Display the **wallpaper** in **tile** format (D)

95. **Apply** this to the desktop (E)

96. Open the **Internet Options** (D)

97. Change the **Homepage** to www.minesec.gov.cm (D)

98. Set the **History** folder to 20 days (D)

99. Change the amount of **Disk space** to use to 60 MB (D)

100.  **Cancel** these selections (E)

**Fill in the Blanks**

1. When you save your file for the first time, you will see the _____ box.

2. _____ option is used for printing the pages.

107

3. The Copy option is present inside the _____ menu bar option.

4. _____ option creates a new file.

5. To type a capital letter, press _____key once to turn it on.

6. _____are small picture buttons that represent programs, folders, files, printer information, computer information etc on your desktop.

7. _____ bar is present at the bottom of the Windows XP desktop.

8. Pressing the left mouse button twice in quick succession is called_____

9. The _____ button is used to reduce the window into a button onto the taskbar.

10. The right side of the Title bar has _____, _____, and _____buttons.

11. The _____can be used for viewing date and time.

12. _____ is an onscreen icon representing your mouse.

13. _____ is used to describe the computer starting up process.

## Glossary Chapter Two

**Aero:** A Windows colour scheme that changes the way Windows itself looks and behaves on your screen.

**Aero Peek:** A Windows 7 tool that allows you to quickly view all open windows and programs in either thumbnail or full screen mode.

**Aero Shake:** A Windows 7 feature that minimizes all windows except the one. Click on the title bar of the window you want to keep open and then drag it back and forth quickly.

**Aero Snap:** A Windows 7 feature that lets you resize a window to half size just by dragging it to a side of the screen.

**Application:** A kind of software used for productivity or to create things (the software that does the work).

**Attachment:** A file that piggybacks onto an e-mail message.

**AutoPlay dialog box:** Appears when you plug a memory card into your PC.

**Bluetooth:** A wireless technology for adding devices to your computer.

**Burning:** Recording content to a CD or DVD.

**Cache:** Also known as the temporary Internet files, the cache contains all Web pages and their components that are downloaded when you subscribe to Web sites or channels.

**Command prompt:** A traditional DOS-like text interface that allows you to input instructions to the computer.

**Compressed file:** A folder containing multiple files that have been packed in such a way that all excess space is eliminated.

**Contiguous files:** In Windows Explorer, these files are shown one right after another.

**Cookies:** Tiny files that are used by Web sites to track your online activity and recognize you whenever you access the site.

**Crop**: To choose a portion of an existing photo and make that portion into the entire photo, omitting the rest of the photo.

**Cursor:** The blinking icon on the computer screen that shows you where the characters you type appear; also called an insertion pointer.

**D3D Score:** The score that the Windows Experience Index gives to your computer's ability to replicate 3D images.

**Default printer:** The primary printer that Windows uses automatically.

**Defrag; defragment:** The process that your computer uses to rearrange the pieces of files and applications on your hard drive so that they are positioned next to each other on the drive, improving performance.

**Desktop:** Windows 7's main screen that shows your program icons, the Start button, and the taskbar.

**Desktop theme:** A collection of settings that control the appearance and behaviour of the various appearance settings in Windows.

**Details pane:** A small strip along the bottom of every folder that lists details about the item you're currently viewing.

**Device Manager:** A Windows tool that shows you the status of all the hardware elements on your PC.

**DNS Server:** A computer that translates Internet addresses you can understand, such as www.dummies.com, into addresses that the Internet can understand, such as 208.215.179.139.

**Double-click rate:** The speed at which you click your mouse button twice. This rate is set in the Mouse Properties dialog box.

**Download:** To copy data (usually an entire file) from a main source to a peripheral device.

**Drag:** To click and hold a mouse button while moving the mouse.

**Drop:** To place an item on the desktop or in a window, after dragging it, by releasing the mouse button.

**E-mail attachment:** A file that is attached to an e-mail message.

**Encryption:** The translation, or scrambling, of data into a secret code.

**Favicon:** The small icon next to a URL address in an Internet browser's address bar.

**File extension:** A three- or four-digit suffix to a filename that tells Windows 7 what program should open the file.

**Firewall:** A software or hardware device designed to block unauthorized intruders from gaining entry to an individual computer or a network.

**Flash drive:** A keychain-size storage unit that saves files on memory cards; you can plug it into your computer and access it like any other external hard drive.

**Flip 3D:** When the Aero color scheme is engaged, this tool allows you to visually scroll through all open applications.

**Folder:** An operating system object that can contain multiple files and other folders.

**Font:** The combination of typeface and other qualities, such as size, pitch, and spacing, that can be applied to characters in a document.

**Frozen:** A state in which your PC does not respond to keyboard or mouse commands; also called locked or locked up.

**Gadget:** A little always-on Windows 7 desktop program, such as the Slide Show, Clock, and RSS Feeds.

**Glass:** A Windows Appearance setting that gives your folders a nearly transparent look

**Grayed out:** Menu options that are currently unavailable.

**Handshake:** The technical term for when two or more pieces of electronic equipment, such as a cell phone and a Bluetooth adapter, first recognize each other.

**Hardware Update Wizard:** A Windows tool that can search for and add hardware to the system.

**Hibernate:** A computer function by which it saves the entire computer's memory (everything the system is doing), then turns the computer off.

**Icon:** A small picture that represents an object or program.

**Insertion point:** The blinking icon that appears on your computer screen at the location where characters you type appear; also called a cursor.

**Internet Service Provider (ISP):** A company that provides access to the Internet.

**Library:** Libraries enable you to group related folders and files together. Windows 7 has four default libraries: Documents, Music, Pictures, and Videos.

**Live file system:** When burning CDs and DVDs, this file system allows you to add and remove files as if the disc were another hard drive.

**Local-area network (LAN):** A computer network that spans a relatively small area. Most LANs are confined to a single building or group of buildings.

**Lock:** The command on the Shutdown menu that suspends computer operations and presents the login screen, but without actually logging off.

**Locked up:** A state in which your PC does not respond to keyboard or mouse commands; also called frozen.

**Log in:** To identify yourself on a computer by entering a username and password.

**Log off:** To tell Windows that you're done using the computer without actually turning off the computer; you must log in to use it again.

**Log on:** To identify yourself on a computer by entering a username and password.

**Log out:** To tell Windows that you're done using the computer without actually turning off the computer; you must log in to use it again.

**Malware:** A type of application that is designed to cause problems (such as file corruption and stealing personal information) to computer systems.

**Master file system:** When burning CDs and DVDs, this setting allows the disc to be read by most computers and players, but it does restrict you to only adding files one time.

**MBR (master boot record) partition:** The portion of the hard drive that contains the operating system.

**Messenger:** A full-featured instant messaging tool – now a part of the Windows Live Essentials pack – that works with any version of Windows as well as Yahoo Messenger.

**MHT:** A Microsoft-proprietary "Web archive" file format.

**Modem:** *Modem* is a contraction of *mo*dulator-*dem*odulator. A device that converts digital data from a computer into analog data for transmission over telephone lines by modulating it into waves. At the other end, a modem converts the analog data back into digital form by demodulating it. Cable modems also convert data but that information may stay in digital form.

**Movie Maker:** Microsoft's video-editing tool, which is now a part of the Windows Live Essentials pack.

**Navigation Pane:** A pane in Windows 7 that contains your most frequently used items. The top portion is Favorite Links; the bottom part is Folders.

**Notebook:** An ultra light laptop built for on-the-road Internet access and word processing.

**Network:** A group of two or more computer systems linked together. Components of a network include a networking adapter, cables, and a hub.

**Network and Sharing Center window:** The window from which you control most of your network settings.

**Paging volume:** The Windows system uses a paging volume to expand the RAM and increase performance.

**Partition:** A drive partition is a way that Windows virtually separates parts of a drive.

**Phishing:** The act of sending an e-mail to a user falsely claiming to be an established legitimate enterprise in an attempt to scam the user into surrendering private information.

**Playlist:** A group of songs with a particular theme often created using Windows Media Player.

**Plug and Play:** A technology that Windows uses to automate hardware installation.

**Plug-in:** A software module that adds a specific feature or service so that you can view a Web site.

**Pop-up window:** A window that suddenly appears (pops up) when you select an option with a mouse or press a special function key in Internet Explorer.

**Power management:** A feature of the operating system that slows or shuts down your computer after a period of inactivity to save power and extend the PC's life.

**Print queue:** The lineup of documents waiting to be output by your printer.

**Problem Steps Recorder (PSR):** A tool that enables you to record exactly what your computer is doing so that you can show whoever you've asked for help.

**Recycle Bin:** A folder on the hard drive where Windows places the files that you delete. Until you empty the Recycle Bin, deleted files can be restored.

**Rip:** To copy music from a CD to your PC. This is often accomplished using Windows Media Player.

**Safe Mode:** A way of entering Windows, primarily for diagnostics and repairs, that bypasses many of the drivers that can cause Windows failures.

**SATA hard drive:** Serial Advanced Technology Attachment: A storage technology that tends to run faster and cooler with simpler connections.

**Scenic Ribbon:** A tab-based interface for Microsoft-based applications, such as WordPad, that contains all the primary commands.

**Screen resolution:** Signifies the number of dots (pixels) on the entire screen.

**Search engine:** A program that searches documents or the Internet for specified keywords and returns a list of the documents or Web pages where the keywords were found.

**Shadow copies:** A type of backup file that automatically saves all previous versions of files.

**Shortcut:** An icon push button, typically placed on your desktop, that allows you to quickly access a program, file, or folder.

**Shortcut menu:** A topic-specific pop-up menu that appears when you right-click an item.

**Shut Down:** The command on the Shutdown menu that powers off the computer.

**Sidebar:** An area along the side of your screen that displays gadgets. These gadgets tell you the time, show pictures, convert money, and feed you the news, among other things.

**Skin:** A visual interface applied to Windows Media Player.

**Sleep**: The command on the Shutdown menu that places the computer into a special, power-saving mode.

**Snipping Tool:** Windows' built-in tool for creating screen shots.

**Spam:** Any unsolicited e-mail.

**Spyware:** Any software that covertly gathers user information through the user's Internet connection without his or her knowledge, usually for advertising purposes.

**Start button:** The button in the lower-left corner of the Windows desktop. By clicking the Start button, you access the Start menu to start programs, adjust Windows settings, find help, and shut down your computer, among other things.

**Start menu:** Allows you to start programs, adjust Windows' settings, find help, and shut down your computer, among other things.

**Sticky Notes:** A Windows 7 accessory that enables you to leave the electronic equivalent of good old-fashioned Post-It notes all over your Windows 7 desktop

**Switch:** In networks, a device that filters and forwards packets between network segments.

**Switch User:** The command on the Shutdown menu that allows another user on the same computer to access his or her account without logging off from your own account.

**Synchronize:** To coordinate a single set of data between two or more devices, automatically copying changes back and forth.

**System image:** A backup file created using Backup and Recovery that can be used to restore the system to exactly the same as it was at the time the image was created – including programs, updates, drivers, and data.

**System Restore:** Uses restore points to return your PC to a point where it works properly.

**Tags:** Part of a file's metadata in which you can give a file a reference name that can be used by Windows 7 and other programs to sort and retrieve files.

**Task Manager:** Windows tool for keeping track of the programs and processes that are currently running.

**Theme:** A Windows 7 theme controls all aspects of the visual workspace – wallpaper (desktop background), colours, icons, screen saver, mouse pointers, and even custom sounds.

**Flash disk:** Another name for a thumb drives, because many flash drives are about the size of a human thumb.

**Title bar:** The thick blue bar that runs across the top of a window.

**Transition:** How movie clips are joined together.

**Uninterruptible power supply, UPS:** A power strip combined with a battery to keep your computer running when the power goes out.

**USB (Universal Serial Bus):** A computer connection that you can use to attach many different kinds of devices and peripherals to a computer.

**User account:** An account that every user must have on a given PC. The account defines the user's privileges and allows the user to customize items, such as the desktop and file settings.

**Username:** The name of your user account.

**Virtual machine:** A software creation that acts and operates like a separate computer within the primary computer.

**Virtual memory:** The portion of your hard drive that Windows uses to expand the available RAM.

**Windows Live Mail:** Microsoft's full-featured free e-mail service – now a part of the Windows Live Essentials pack.

**Windows Media Player:** Software that lets you collect, play, and share your music.

**Windows Movie Maker:** Software that lets you import your video and photos, edit them into a movie, and save your creation to your PC, a DVD, or a CD.

**Windows Photo Gallery:** Software that lets you easily sort through your photos by clicking different words, dates and ratings listed on the Navigation Pane.

**Windows Registry:** A portion of the Windows system that contains a wide variety of information that instructs Windows how to handle registered applications.

**Windows Update:** Allows Microsoft to automatically send you patches for Windows 7.

**WinSAT (Windows System Assessment Tool):** The measurement tool that Windows7 uses to assess your system's capabilities and to create the WEI index for your PC.

**Wizard:** A Windows tool that automates common processes, such as adding software or setting up a network.

# CHAPTER THREE
## WORD PROCESSING
### Introduction to Microsoft Word

Microsoft Word allows you to produce professional documents quickly and effectively. You can use Microsoft Word create things like; simple letters, reports, manuals, newsletters, fax messages, banners, brochures, etc.

**Microsoft Office** – This is a package (CD or DVD) that contains the programs of Microsoft Corporation. Related software programs sometimes sold bundled together as **software suite.** So the package containing Microsoft Office is a software suite. When you purchase Microsoft (MS) Office license you basically purchase the right to install and use Microsoft Word, Microsoft Excel, Microsoft Power Point, Microsoft Access, Microsoft Publisher, Microsoft FrontPage etc.

- The software suite Microsoft Office 2000 contains Microsoft Word 2000, Microsoft Excel 2000, Microsoft Power Point 2000, Microsoft Access 2000, Microsoft Publisher 2000, and Microsoft FrontPage 2000 etc.

- The software suite Microsoft (MS) Office XP contains MS Word XP, MS Excel XP, MS Power Point XP, MS Access XP, MS Publisher XP and FrontPage XP etc.

- The software suite Microsoft Office 2003 contains MS Office Word 2003, MS Office Excel 2003, MS Office Power Point 2003, MS Office Access 2003, MS Office Publisher 2003 and FrontPage 2003 etc.

- The software suite Microsoft Office 2007 contains MS Office Word 2007, MS Office Excel 2007, MS Office Power Point 2007, MS Office Access 2007, MS Office Publisher 2007 and FrontPage 2007 etc.

- The Software suite Microsoft Office 2010 contains MS Office Word 2010, MS Office Excel 2010, MS Office Power Point 2010, MS Office Access 2010, MS Office Publisher 2010 and FrontPage 2010 etc.

**Starting Microsoft Word**

➢ Click on Start button

➢ Select All Programs,

➢ Select Microsoft Office,

➢ Select Microsoft Word

➢ The Microsoft Word window appears displaying a blank document

OR

·If the Microsoft Word icon is found on the desktop double-click to start MS Word.

**The Microsoft Office Word 2003 Window (see page 66)**

- The title bar identifies the current application and shows the filename of the current document e.g. in our example the filename is *Document 1*

- The menu bar contain list of menus with related commands.

- The control menu buttons composed of the program control buttons – used to size and close the word window;

and the document control buttons used to size and close the current document window.

- The standard toolbar contains buttons used to activate frequently used commands.
- The select browse object button that allow moving quickly through the document.
- The formatting toolbar contains buttons to activate common fonts and paragraph formatting commands.
- The horizontal ruler adjusts margins, tabs, and column width; vertical ruler appears in Print Layout view.
- The document window is the area where you enter text and graphics.
- The document view buttons to left of horizontal bar show the document in five different views: Normal, Web Layout, Print Layout, Reading Layout, and Outline views.
- The status bar is the horizontal area below the document window and provides information on the current state of what you are viewing in window and any other contextual information.
- The mouse pointer changes shape depending on its location on screen.
- The insertion point indicates the location where characters will be inserted or deleted.
- The scroll bars shift text vertically and horizontally on the screen so that you can see different parts of the document.
- The scroll box helps you move quickly to other pages of your document.

## Entering Text in a Window

Microsoft Word let you type text into your document easily.

· The flashing line on your window is called the **cursor** or **insertion point**. It indicates where the text you type will appear. During typing, Microsoft Word automatically wraps text to the next line. You can Press Enter when you want to start a new line or paragraph.

Microsoft Word underlines wrong spellings with **wavy redlines** and wrong grammar with **wavy green lines.** Note that, local names and other names which are not found in the dictionary of Microsoft Word are also underlined with wavy redlines.

The Microsoft Word 2003 screen display several bars to help you perform tasks quickly.

i.) Standard Toolbar – contains icons and buttons to help you quickly select

commonly use commands such as **Open, New, Save, Print** etc

ii.) Formatting Toolbar – helps you quickly select formatting and layout

features such as bold, underline, font type, font size, italics etc.

iii.) Ruler: Allows you to set your margins, change Tab stops using the Marker.

**Note:** The Standard toolbar, formatting toolbar, drawing toolbar are shortcuts to the main menu. For example instead of;

119

Selecting the word to use boldface

· Click on Format menu

· Select Font

· The font dialog box appears

· Click on Bold in the font style list

· Click on Ok

You can just select the word to boldface and click on **B** on the formatting tool bar. Most of those who begin by using shortcuts get choked-up because if the toolbar is no more there they will not know what to do. It is a better idea to start with the main menu before coming to use toolbar shortcuts. It is just like knowing the main road before using the shortcut in case the shortcut is blocked you still find your way.

**Note** that you can create your own toolbars after knowing the menus and select the commands you will use most often and place on your tool bar.

**Create a tool bar named Luma**

**To do this,**

· Click on Tools menu

· Select Customize

· The customize dialog box appears

· Click on Toolbars Tab

· Click on New button

· In the New Tool bar dialog box that appears

· Type Luma in Toolbar name box
· Click on OK

The Luma Tool bar is created.

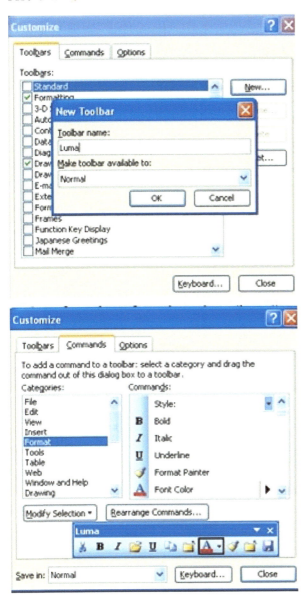

In the customize dialog box above to the right, the Commands Tab is selected and you can pick and drag commands after choosing categories to the Luma tool bar as I have done.

If you will like editing, formatting, viewing, managing files with toolbar buttons then simply create your own and put the commands you will use most often on it.

Then you will notice it is important to know the main menu from where these shortcuts lead than just knowing the shortcuts without knowing the source.

**Note:** Microsoft Word 2007 makes it very easy for you to add commands which you will used most often to the **Customize Quick Access Toolbar** instead of creating your own toolbar as above and adding commands or using commands on the Standard, Formatting, Drawing toolbars in Microsoft Word 2003.

To do this;

· Click on **Office button**

· Click on **Word Options** button

· Click on **Customize**

· Select **All Commands** from the Choose commands from dropdown list

· Select a command and click **Add** to add the command to the Customize Quick Access Toolbar. The secret you should note concerning Microsoft Word is that all its versions have all the commands built in the program and you can access them using the **customize command**. In the future when you meet any new version just look for the **Customize Command** and pick all the commands you will need to use during your workday and make them accessible to you.

The Microsoft Word 2007 Word Options dialog box is shown below.

**Selecting Text**

Before performing tasks in Microsoft Word you must select text, selected text appears on your screen in video reverse.

*To select a word double click any where over the word you want to select.

* To deselect a word click outside the selected area

* To select a line, position the mouse pointer on left margin and click.

* To select a sentence – press and hold Ctrl while clicking anywhere over

  the sentence and then release Ctrl key.

* To select a paragraph – position the mouse pointer anywhere over the

  paragraph and then quickly click three times – treble click.

* To select the whole document, Click Edit menu, Select All or press

Ctrl+A. See more methods on selecting text with keystrokes in windows

in the table: **Editing Keys for Textboxes and other Text(see page36)**

## Status Bar MS Office 2003 window

Page 1 — The page displayed on your screen

Sec 1 – The section displayed on your screen

1/18 – Page displayed on screen and the total number of pages in the document.

At 14.7cm – Distance from the top of the page to the insertion point.

Ln – Number of lines from the top of the page to the insertion point.

Col – Number of characters from left margin to the insertion point including spaces.

## Status bar MS Office 2007 Window

The buttons to the right on this status bar are the viewing options; Print layout, Full Screen Reading, Web layout, outline and draft. They offer Microsoft Word ways to display a document on screen and each of these views is designed to make editing tasks easier.

These various views have no effect on the content of your document. They affect only the way the document appears on the screen.

## Zooming the Screen

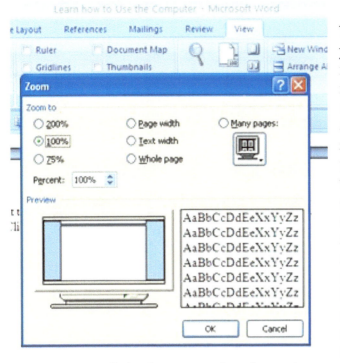

You can zoom your screen to facilitate reading on screen. You can also decrease zoom percentage to view an entire document at once. You can zoom using the zoom in, zoom out on the zoom bar at the right end of the status bar or the zoom dialog box below. Click the zoom level on the status bar to open the dialog box.

## Full Screen View

This is the maximum amount of screen view area. None of the scroll bars is displayed. Your document occupies the entire screen. You can enter and edit text in this view using the vital keyboard strokes. To turn on full screen view, click on View menu, select full screen (for Word 2003) and Click **Office button, View Tab** Full Screen Reading Microsoft Word 2007.

**Setting your Page.** Before you create a banner, brochure, fax message etc you should choose the paper size which you will use before you begin and set its margins. To do this:

* Click on File menu     * Select Page Setup
* The Page Setup dialog box appears
* Via the Margins tab, set your margins (top, bottom, left, right, gutter),
  Orientation (Portrait or Landscape)
* Click on Ok
* Via the Paper tab, choose paper size from the paper size drop down list
  (A4, A5, Letter, A3, Envelope Dl, Envelope C5 etc)
* Click on Ok

**Creating a New Document**
* Click on File menu
* Click on New
* The New Document dialog box appears
 * Click on Blank document
To create a document based on a template or wizard click the button XLM document.

**Saving a New Unnamed Document**

* Click on File menu

* Click on Save As

* The Save As dialog box appears

* In the Save in drop down list box, choose the drive or folder into which

  you want to save the document

* In the File name box, type the name of the document

* Click on Save button

**Note**: In the Save as type drop down list box, choose Word document, Rich Text Format etc depending on whether you will subsequently export the file to another program.

**Save a Document (Ctrl+S)**

* Click on File menu

* Select Save

Or

* Click on Save icon found on the standard tool bar

**Microsoft Office Word**

⚠ Do you want to save the changes to Document8?

[ Yes ]   [ No ]   [ Cancel ]

**Closing a Document**

* Click on File menu

* Select Close

If you have not saved before with a new name, a dialog box will appear asking you "Do you want to save the changes you made to document8?

**Note**: All the commands in Microsoft Office 2003 under File menu are accessed in Microsoft Office 2007 under the Office button, Microsoft Office 2010 and 2013 under the File Tab.

Click Yes to save the changes.

Click No to ignore the changes.

Click Cancel to escape.

**Exiting Microsoft Word**

* Click on File menu

* Select Exit

It is important to exit all programs before you shut down your computer.

**Opening a Document (Ctrl + O)**

* Click on File menu

* Select Open

* The Open dialog box appears

* Using the Look in box, select folder or drive in which your document was saved.

* Highlight the document name

* Click on Open button

You can also open a document as read only, in browser, with transform or open and repair using the drop down arrow on the Open button.

If your computer is connected to the Internet, you can open a document located at an http site on the World Wide Web.

**Switch Between Documents**

To display a list of all opened documents

* Click on Window menu

* Click the name of document you want

* The document name is displayed on the title bar

You can also use the taskbar button to switch between several documents.

**Editing with Microsoft Word**

**Copy Text (Ctrl + C)**

* Select the text you want copied

* Click on Edit Menu

* Select Copy

Or

* Pres Ctrl + C on the keyboard

* Position the cursor where you want to place the text

* Click on Edit menu

* Select Paste

Or

* Press Ctrl + V

To copy text means to make a duplicate of the text and the original text remains intact.

**The Cut Command (Ctrl + X)**

* Select the text you want to cut
* Click on Edit menu
* Select cut

Or

* Press Ctrl + X

The **Undo Command (Ctrl + Z)**

* Click on Edit menu
* Select Undo

Or

* Press Ctrl + Z

**The Redo Command (Ctrl + Y)**

* Click on Edit menu
* Select Repeat (last action)

**Check Errors of Spellings and Grammar**

Microsoft Word provides two ways to check errors of spellings and grammar. As you type, Microsoft Word automatically checks your document and underline possible spelling and grammatical errors. To correct an error, right-click to display a shortcut menu, and then select the correction you want.

**Automatically Check Spellings and Grammar as you type**

* Click on Tools menu, Select Options and then click the Spelling and Grammar tab
* Select the spelling as you type and check grammar as you type check boxes.

If the option you want appears grayed out, it is unavailable, and you need to install the appropriate spelling and grammar checker.

* Uncheck the Hide spelling errors in this document check box
* Click Ok
* To correct an error, right-click a word with a wavy red underline, and then click the correction you want on the shortcut menu.

To use additional spelling and grammar options, click Spelling and Grammar on the shortcut menu. You can edit the error directly in the document.

**Check Spellings, Grammar, and Readability all at once**

* Click on Tools menu, Select Options and then Click Spelling and Grammar tab.
* Select the check grammar with spellings and show readability statistics check boxes.
* Click Ok

When you finish creating a document, you can have Word search the document for spelling and grammatical errors. To do t his,

* Click on Tools menu
* Select Spelling and Grammar
* The spelling and grammar dialog box appears

* Select one suggestion by clicking on it
* Click change
* Click ignore to skip the error
* Click ignore all to skip error and all occurrences of the error
* Click add to add a new word to the dictionary of MS Word
* Click change all after selecting one suggestion to change all occurrences of the error in the document
* Click auto correct to correct the word automatically

**Using the Thesaurus**

Thesaurus is used to look for synonyms and antonyms of words. Select the word you want to replace with another synonym.

- Click on Tools menu
- Select Language
- Thesaurus
- The Thesaurus dialog box appears
- To replace the word in the document, click Replace
- Click Cancel to close the dialog box

Thesaurus can be used to find synonyms for the word in the Looked up button. This procedure may be repeated until a suitable synonym is found. The Thesaurus keeps a list of all the words you have looked up. To return to the previous word open the looked up list box by clicking the arrow at the end of the box. Words which you have previously looked up are displayed and the required word can be chosen from the list.

Let's look for the synonyms of the word "nice"

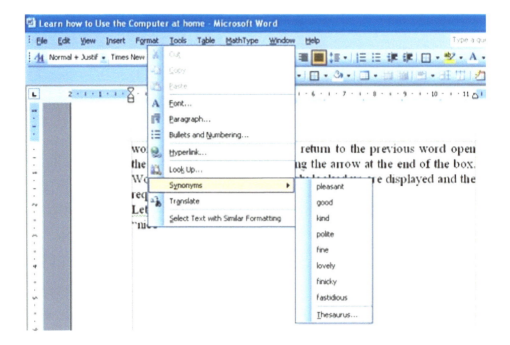

## Find and Replace

You can use the find command to locate words or phrases in your document.

➤ Click on Edit menu

➤ Select Find

➤ The Find and Replace dialog box appears

➤ In the Find what box, type the name or phrase you want to find

➤ Click Find next to start searching

➤ To find next marching word, click Find next

➤ Select the Replace tab, in the Replace with box,

type word to replace word you have found.

➤ Click Replace to replace the word

➤ Click Replace All to replace the word and all occurrences of the word in the document

➤ Click Cancel to close the dialog box

• Click Go To tab

• Enter page number

• Click next to move to that page

**AutoCorrect**

– Click on Tools menu

– Select AutoCorrect

– The Auto correct dialog box appears

– Auto correct

corrects every wrong word, replaces them in the text as you are typing e.g. it replaces abouta to about, beleive to believe etc.

Note that you can normally add words and corrections in AutoCorrect so that they will subsequently correct as you type. Other Auto correct facilities include;

Correction to capitals at the beginning of a sentence, capitalization of first letters of names of days, months of the year, correction of accidental usage of caps lock key etc.

**Formatting**

It helps to change the appearance of a document to make it look attractive. You can either format characters or entire paragraphs.

**Formatting Characters**

**To format characters**

* Select the text you want to format it characters
* Click on Format menu
* Select font
* In the font dialog box that appears choose font type, font style, font size, font colour, underline style etc
* Select Font Effects (subscript, superscript, outline etc)
* Click the Ok button at the end of thess procedures

In the example in the dialog box above, you have chosen font colour red, underline style dashes, underline colour black and Effects shadow. When you click on Ok button the word **FORMATTING** will be formatted with these specifications.

**Paragraph Formatting**

Paragraphs are either denoted by an indent (first line) set in from the left margin or by use of spaces between them.

*Select the text you want to format as paragraph

*Click on Format menu

*Select Paragraph

*The Paragraph dialog box appears

*Choose alignment (left, centre, right, justify)

*Specify spacing before and after paragraphs

*Under the line space drop down list box choose line spacing

*Click on Ok button.

**Line Spacing**

Line spacing determines the amount of vertical space between lines of text. Word uses single line spacing by default. The line spacing you select will affect all lines of text in the selected paragraph or the paragraph that contains the insertion point.

| This option | Results in |
|---|---|
| Single | Line spacing for each line that accommodates the largest font in that line plus a small amount of extra space. The amount of extra space varies depending on the font used. |
| 1.5 Lines | Line spacing for each line that is one-and-one-half times that of a single line spacing. For example, if 10-point text is spaced at 1.5 lines, the line spacing is approximately 15 points |

| | |
|---|---|
| Double | Line spacing for each line is twice that of single line spacing. For example, in double–spaced lines of 10-point text, the line spacing is approximately 20 points. |
| At Least | Minimum line spacing that Word can adjust to accommodate larger font sizes or graphics that would not otherwise fit within the specified spacing. |
| Exactly | Fixed line spacing that Word does not adjust. This option makes all lines evenly spaced. |
| Multiple | Line spacing that is increased or decreased by a percentage that you specify. For example, setting line spacing to a multiple of 1.2 will increase the space by 20 percent. Setting the line spacing at a multiple of 2 is equivalent to setting the line spacing to double. In the At box, type or select the line spacing you want. The default is three lines |
| At | The amount of line spacing you select. This option is available only if you select At Least, Exactly, or Multiple in the Line Space box. |

## Indent Paragraphs

When you increase or decrease indenting, you change the distance of the text from the margins. When you create a hanging indent, you offset an element, such as a bullet, number or word to the left of the first line of text

**Set left and right indents by using the ruler**

Select the paragraphs you want to indent or set off from the left or right margins.

- To change the left indent of the first line of text, drag the first line marker at the top of the ruler.
- To change the indent of the second line of text, drag the left indent marker
- To change the left indent for all lines of text within a paragraph, drag the box underneath the left indent marker.
- To change the right indent for all lines of text, drag the right indent marker.

**Set the left indent by using the Tab key**

* Click on Tools menu, Options, and the Smart Paragraph check box is selected on Edit tab
* Click in front of the paragraph of text
* Press the Tab key

**Note**: to remove indent, press Backspace

**Change the Horizontal alignment of text**

**Align text with the left margin**

Select the text you want to align left

* Click on Format menu
* Select Paragraph
* In the Paragraph dialog box that appears, under Indents and Spacing tab

   \*   Select **left** from the Alignment drop down list

**Center text**

Select text you want to center

   \*   Click on Format menu

   \*   Select Paragraph

   \*   In the Paragraph dialog box that appears, under Indents and Spacing tab

   \*   Select **Centered** from the Alignment drop down list

**Align text with the right margin**

Select the text you want to align with the right margin

\* Click on Format menu

\* Select Paragraph

\* In the Paragraph dialog box that appears, under Indents and Spacing tab

\* Select **right** from the Alignment drop down list

**Justify text**

Select the text you want to justify.

   \*   Click on Format menu

   \*   Select Paragraph

   \*   In the Paragraph dialog box that appears, under Indents and Spacing tab

   \*   Select **justified** from the Alignment drop down list

**Keep lines together**

   \*   Select the paragraphs that contain lines you want to keep together

   \*   Click on Format menu, Paragraph

\*  Check the Keep with next check box via the Line and Page Breaks tab on the Paragraph dialog box that appears.

**Paragraph Indenting Vs Page Margins**

Be careful not to confuse indenting paragraphs with setting the left and right margins. Margin settings determine the overall width of the main text area in other words, the space between the text and the edge of the page. When you indent a paragraph, you specify the distance of the text from the margins. By using indenting, you can also offset selected paragraphs from other text in your document.

You will easily indent several paragraphs to the same indentation in a large document by using Format menu, Paragraph, Indentation, Specifying left and right in the boxes and clicking on Ok.

**Borders and Shading**

There are two types of borders i.e. there are borders that you can apply to paragraphs, lines etc and those that you can apply to the whole page or pages

**Borders**

· Select the paragraph or line of text to which you want to apply a border

· Click on Format menu

· Select Borders and Shading

· The Borders and Shading dialog box appears

- Under the Borders tab, choose setting that you desire (Box, Shadow, 3D, Custom)
- Choose type of border you want
- From the Apply to drop down list choose Paragraph to apply border to paragraph or selected text to apply to text you have selected.
- Click on Ok button.

**Page Borders**

**Note: In the case of page borders you don't need to select the text**

- Click on Format menu
- Select Borders and Shading
- The Borders and Shading dialog box appears
- Under the Page Border tab, use the Art drop down list
- Select a border you desire
- Click on Ok button

**To Remove Borders/Page Border**

- Select the text
- Click on Format menu
- Select Borders and Shading
- The Borders and Shading dialog box appears
- Under the Borders or Page Border tab click on None.

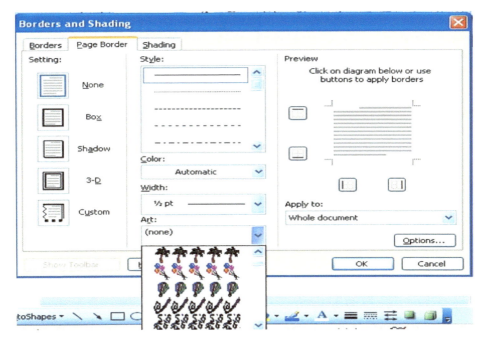

## Shading

· Select the paragraph to which you want shading applied
· Click on Format menu
· Select Borders and Shading

· The Borders and Shading dialog box appears

· Under the Shading tab, use the Fill colours and Patterns style to fill with colours and patterns

· Click on Ok button

## Bullets and Numbering

## Bullets

You can add bullets and numbers before commencing to type or after typing your text. To do this,

· Select the text to which you want to add bullets

· Click on Format menu

· Select Bullets and Numbers

· The Bullets and Numbers dialog box appears

- Click on the Bulleted tab, Choose bullet type you desire and click on Ok button.

**Note**: If the bullet nature you desire is not found under Bulleted tab in the Bullets and Numbers dialog box, select any bullet nature under Bulleted tab, Click on customize to go to the Customize Bulleted List dialog box. Set font, character, picture, and specify bullet position from the left margin in the Indent at box.

### Numbers

- Select the text to which you want to add numbers
- Click on Format menu
- Select Bullets and Numbers
- The Bullets and Numbers dialog box appears
- Click on the Numbered tab, Choose number format you desire and click on Ok button.

**Note**: If the number format you desire is not found under Numbered tab in the Bullets and Numbers dialog box, select any number format under Numbered tab, Click on customize to go to the Customize Numbered List dialog box.

Choose number format, style, and position. Enter start number in the Start at box, enter alignment, indentation and tab in the Aligned at, Indent at and Tab space after boxes respectively and Click on Ok button.

### Outline Numbering

- Select the text to which you want to add outline numbers

- Click on Format menu
- Select Bullets and Numbers
- The Bullets and Numbers dialog box appears
- Click on the Outline Numbered tab, Choose number format you desire and click on Ok button.

**Note**: If the Outline number format you desire is not found under Outline Numbered tab in the Bullets and Numbers dialog box, select any number format under Outline Numbered tab, Click on customize to go to the Customize Outline Numbered List dialog box. Choose outline number format, style, and position. Enter start number in the Start at box, enter alignment, indentation and tab in the Aligned at, Indent at and Tab space after boxes respectively and Click on Ok button.

### Symbols Microsoft Word 2003

You can add symbols to your document in the following ways:

- Position the cursor where you want the symbol to appear
- Click on Insert menu
- Select Symbol
- The Symbol dialog box appears
- Via the font drop down list choose a symbol category, click on the symbol you want and click on insert.
- Click Cancel button to come out of the symbol dialog box Or

- Use the Alt key with the combination of three numeric keys to insert symbols e.g. Alt+130 = é    Alt+136 = ê Alt+133 = à etc.

If you have MathType installed on your computer, the MathType menu appears on the menu bar as in my menu bar example below. So you can insert and type mathematical equations easily with MathType incorporated into Microsoft Word.

The Equation under Insert menu has been incorporated into Office 2007 to enable you insert more mathematical symbols or to build up your own mathematical equations. The Equation command is not available in Microsoft Office 2003 and to build up your own equation you need to install MathType.

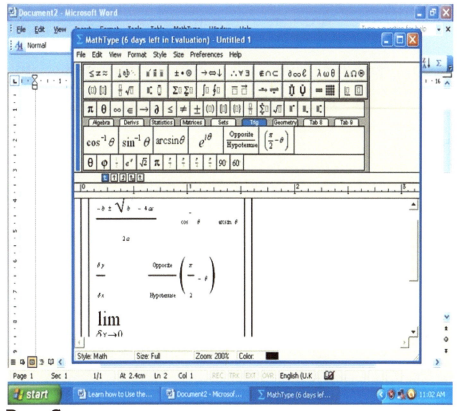

## Drop Cap

- Select the letter you want to format as drop cap

- Click on Format menu

- Select drop cap

- In the Drop Cap dialog box that appears, select Dropped

- Choose font, number of lines to drop, distance from text and click on Ok.

## Columns within Microsoft Word 2003

You can add columns to your document before you begin or after completing typing the document.

- Select the text to which you want to add columns

- Click on Format menu

145

- Columns
- The Columns dialog box appears. Under Presets choose number of columns (2, 3 etc) or in the number of columns box, type number of columns you want.
- Check line between check box to put a line between the columns
- Uncheck the equal column width if you want columns to be of different sizes
- In the Width and Spacing boxes, specify the width and spacing for the columns.
- Click on Ok.

**Capitalize Text**

You can format text as all capital letters or as all small capital letters.

**Change the case of text**

- Select the text you want to change
- Click on Format menu
- Select change case
- The change case dialog box appears
- Check the capitalization option you want (Sentence, lowercase, UPPERCASE, Title Case, tOGGLE cASE)
- Click on Ok button.

**Graphics or Pictures within Microsoft Word 2003**

You can use auto shapes to create graphics yourself in Microsoft Word or you can use the Insert Menu, Picture and get graphics from the Clip Art Gallery. If you scan a graphic and store on your disk, you can import this same file and use to work with in Microsoft Word. Also, there are static programs like Print Artist, Photoshop available in the market for you to buy which contains graphics which you can import and use in Microsoft Word.

Now let's insert a picture from Clip Art

· Click on Insert menu

· Picture

· Clip Art

· The Clip Art dialog box appears

· Type people in the Search for box

· Drag the picture you desire to the work area

**Format Graphics or Pictures**

· Select the picture or graphic you want to format

· Click on Format menu

· Select Picture

· The Format Picture dialog box appears

· Use the Format picture dialog box or picture tool bar to format your picture depending on what you are doing.

· You can also use the drawing tool bar to draw AutoShapes and format in Microsoft Word. This enables you to create illustrations and logos of your choice.

**Print Preview**

It shows exactly how your document will look like when it is printed. To preview a document,

· Click on File menu

· Select Print Preview

· The Print preview window appears

Or

· Click the Print preview icon on the standard toolbar in MS Office 2003

If you are using MS Office 2007 Click the **Microsoft Office Button** 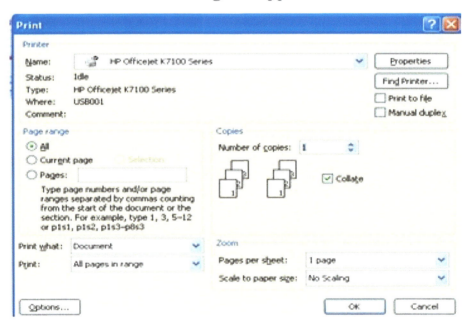, point to the arrow next to **Print**, and then click **Print Preview**.

**Printing a Document**

· Click the **Microsoft Office Button** point to **Print,** Click **Print.** The Print dialog box appears.

Choose one of the following options:

**All** – Print every page in the document

**Current page** – Print the page containing the insertion point or cursor

**Pages** – Print pages you specify e.g. enter page numbers and/or page ranges separated by commas counting from the start of the document or the section e.g. 1, 3,5–12 or p1s1, p1s2, p1s3–p8s3.

**Selection** – Print text you have selected.

Click on **Properties** button to set preferences in the Advanced, Printing Shortcuts, Features and colour tabs.

**Tabs Stops**

They are used to represent text or numbers as lists or columns. Don't use the space bar to format or align text with Word Processors. It impedes formatting and when printed out, it will not appear in columns.

**Default Tabs Stops**

The simplest way of creating text that is lined up in columns is to use Tabs Stops. MS Word provides default Tabs Stops at approximately 1.27cm (½ inch). Text can be aligned at this Tab Stop by pressing the Tab key on the keyboard. Default Tabs Stops can be changed by clicking Format menu, Tabs and then making the appropriate changes in the Tabs dialog box that appears.

**Exercise**

| Days | Time | Activities |
|---|---|---|
| Monday | 7:30am | Open |
| Tuesday | 3:00pm | Prayer Meeting |
| Wednesday | 8:00am | Letter writing |
| Thursday | 10:00pm | Studies |
| Friday | 4:00pm | Sports |

| Saturday | 6:00am | Laundry |
|----------|--------|---------|
| Sunday | 8:15am | Holy Mass |

1. Type the text above, use font type Times New Roman, font size 14, Tabs Stops 1.5cm, Save As **Exercise.**

## Footnotes and Endnotes

They are notes of reference and explanation or comments. A word in the main text can be marked with a foot or end note. In a nutshell footnotes are an extra piece of information that is printed at the bottom of a page in a book. Footnotes appear at the end of the page while endnotes appear at the end of the document. To insert footnotes, position cursor where you want the footnote or endnote to appear, Click on Insert Menu, **Footnote**, in the footnote dialog box that appears choose format, numbering and click on Ok. The footnote shortcut is similar in all Microsoft Word versions.

## Set Password for a Document

· Click on **File** menu

· Select **Save As,** in the Save As dialog box that appears choose folder or drive where you want to save, click on tools dropdown list

· Choose general options and in the dialog box that appears, type password to open and modify.

- Click on Ok button
- Re-enter password to open and modify and click on Ok button.
- Save your document and close.

**Headers and Footers**

They are primarily used in printed documents. However, if you have created a web page that uses frames, you can also add a header or footer to it.

- Click on View menu
- Select Header and Footer
- To create a header, enter text or graphic in header area.
- To create footer, enter text or graphic in footer area. In Microsoft

Word version 2007 access headers and footers via Office button or from **Insert Tab.**

**Index Entry**

An index is an alphabetical list of important words or phrases that appear in your document alongside the respective page numbers. An index is usually found at the end of a document. To create an index, you must first go through the document and mark all important words and phrases as index entries using the Mark Index Entry dialog box and then insert the index via Index dialog box.

To insert index entries in a book or document, do the following:

- Select the word you want to mark for index entries
- Click on Insert menu, Reference, Index and Tables

· The Index and Tables dialog box appears

· Via the Index Tab, click **Mark Entry**

· The Mark Entry Index dialog box appears with selected word in the main entry box

· Select a new word and click on an empty part of the Mark Entry Index dialog box for the word to appear in the main entry box

· The dialog box stays open so that you can mark multiple entries

· When done, placed the insertion point on a new page

· Via the Index and Tables dialog box choose formats e.g. Classic, fancy, modern etc

· Click on Ok button to insert a table of index entries

## CHAPTER FOUR

## Standard Microsoft (MS) Word 2007

· You can display non-printing characters on the screen. This may be useful if you have received a document and are not sure how it is formatted. Click on the **Office Button** and select the **Word Options** button.

This will display the **Word Options** dialog box. Select the **Display** button and you will see the following options.

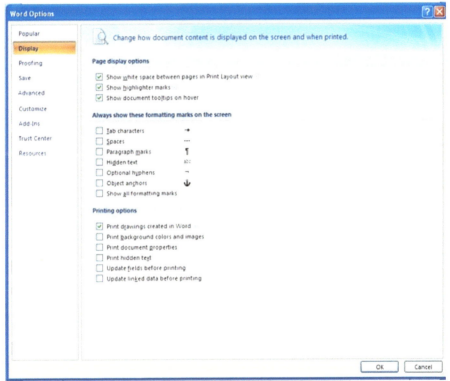

· If you clicked on the **Tab Characters** check box, when you click on the **OK** button you would see any Tab characters displayed in your document as a right-pointing arrow. In the same way you could display spaces, paragraph marks and a range of other options. Experiment with ticking or checking all these options and observe the effect on the display of your document.

· Before continuing, turn these features off again.

### Modifying Word Options

·       In addition to modifying the display options, you can also customize a range of other options. Just take a look at what is possible. If you have time use the Help available within Microsoft Word to get more information about these options.

### Popular Options:

### Proofing Options:

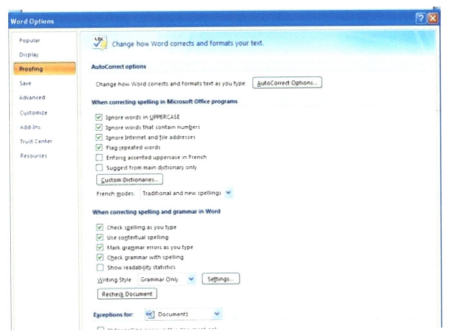

## Save Options:

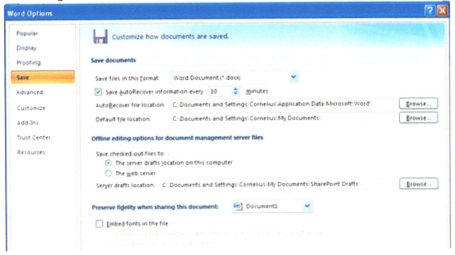

## Advanced Options:

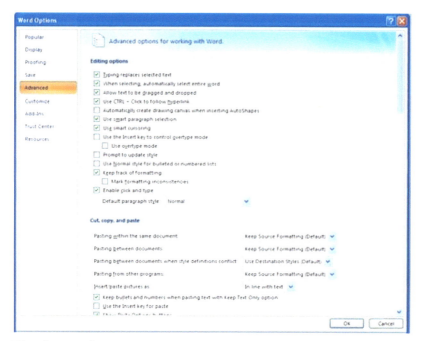

## Hyphenation

· If a word within a document is too large to fit at the end of a line then normally Microsoft Word will automatically drop down to the next line and start the word on this new line i.e. by default the word is not hyphenated.

· Microsoft Word contains a **Hyphenation** option allowing you to automatically or manually hyphenate the text. You can also set the size of the hyphenation zone at the end of a line which determines the maximum amount of space between a word and the right hand margin without hyphenating the word.

### Setting Automatic Hyphenation

· Type a document and save it as **Hyphenation**

. Close the document **Hyphenation**

· Open the document called **Hyphenation**.

· To turn on automatic hyphenation click on the **Page Layout** tab. Click on the **Hyphenation** button (located within the **Page Setup** section under the **Page Layout** tab) and then on the **Automatic** command.

### Hyphenation Options

· Click on the **Page Layout** tab. Click on the **Hyphenation** button and then on the **Hyphenation Options** command. This will display the **Hyphenation** dialog box.

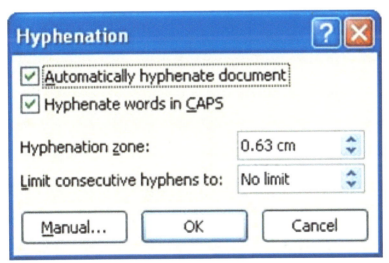

· Use the **Hyphenation zone** section of the dialog box to set the amount of space you want for the hyphenation zone. Experiment again.

· Save your changes and close the document.

## Applying Subscript and Superscript Text Formatting

· Type a document and save as **Text effects**.

· Close the document **Text effects**.

· Open the document called **Text effects**.

· Type in Einstein's famous equation: **E=MC2**

· You have typed in the text as above, but we need to format the equation so that it looks like the illustration below. The **2** needs to be formatted using superscript.

· To format the equation properly, select the **2** in the equation, as illustrated. $E = MC2$

Click on the **Home** tab and from within the **Font** section, click on the **Superscript** icon. $x^2$

· You will see the equation formatted as illustrated below.

$E = MC^2$

Next we will apply subscript formatting to the chemical formula for water.

·        Type in the following: **H2O**

· We need to format the **2** within the formula using subscript. Select the number **2**.

· Click on the **Home** tab and from within the **Font** section, click on the **Subscript** icon. $x_2$

· You will see the equation formatted as illustrated below
$H_2O$

Format the other lines of text within the document as directed, using other text effects, such as strikethrough, shadow effects etc.

· Save your changes and close the document.

**Inserting Special Characters and Symbols**

The keyboard can only contain a limited number of different letters, numbers and other items such as alternative currency symbols and the at (@) sign. You can insert many more symbols and special characters if you wish, examples of which include:

Type a document and save as **Symbols**. Close the document **Symbols**. Open the document called **Symbols**. This document contains a number of symbols and special characters. Click to the right of the first picture of a symbol and then click on the **Insert** tab. You will see the **Symbol** command as illustrated.

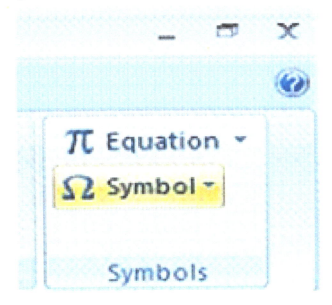

Clicking on the **Symbol** command will display a drop down list of symbol options, as illustrated below.

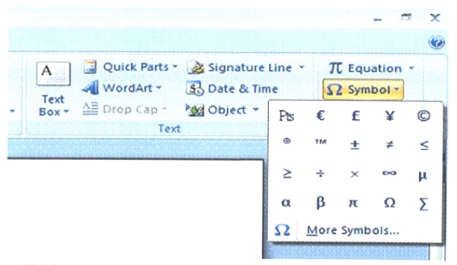

· Clicking on any one of these will insert the symbol that you clicked on (at the position you place your cursor or Insertion point).

· Clicking on **More Symbols**, will display additional symbols and options, as illustrated underneath.

If you click on the **Special Characters** tab within this dialog box, you will see a list of special characters. As you can see, many of these special symbols have a shortcut key displayed to the right of the special character, within the dialog box. These can be useful if you need to insert a special character on a regular basis.

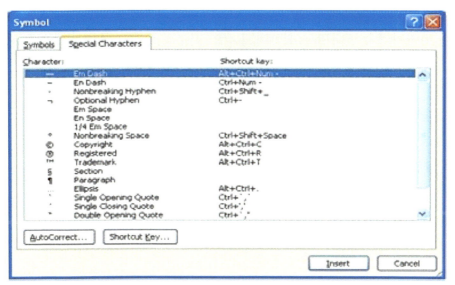

Work through the exercises contained within the **Symbols** document. When you have finished, save your changes and close the document.

### AutoCorrect Options

· Microsoft Word has an AutoCorrect facility that allows common typing errors to be automatically corrected. For instance if you type in '**teh**' instead of '**the**', Microsoft Word will automatically correct your spelling error.

To open the **AutoCorrect** dialog box, click on the **Office Button** (top-left of your screen). Click on the **Word Options** button at the bottom of the dialog box.

Click on the **Proofing** option, and then click on the **AutoCorrect Options** button.

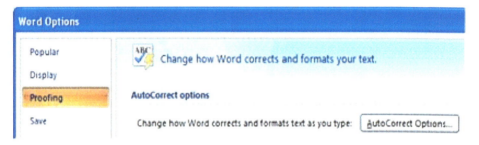

This will display the **AutoCorrect** dialog box.

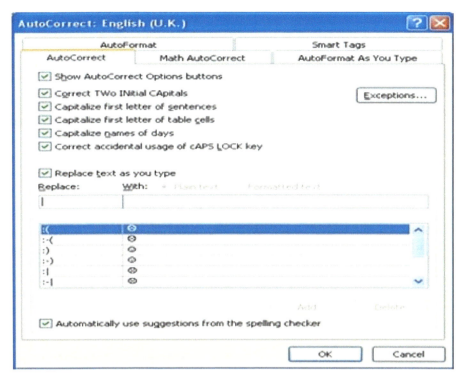

· As you can see this has a number of options such as the ability to correct words where you have accidentally typed in the first two letters in capitals.

· It will also automatically capitalize the first letter within a sentence and also the first letter within a table cell and the days of the week. A very useful feature is to automatically correct the effect of accidentally pressing the Caps Lock key.

· In the lower part of the dialog box is a scrollable section which tells you what Microsoft Word will act on and change automatically. For instance if you wanted to insert a smiling face symbol (J) you would type in a colon, followed by dash, followed by a closing bracket. As you scroll down this list you will see examples of incorrectly spelt words that Microsoft Word will automatically correct for you.

· Add some words that you commonly spell incorrectly, into the **Replace** section of the dialog box, along with the correct spelling in the **With** section of the dialog box.

### AutoFormat as you type

· You can use the '**AutoFormat As You Type**' feature to automatically format as you type text into your document.
1/4 automatical changes to ¼. For instance a fraction such as a half or a quarter can be typed in and automatically reformatted as illustrated below.
To open the **AutoFormat** dialog box, click on the **Office Button** and then click on the **Word Options** button at the bottom of the dialog box.

Click on the **Proofing** option, and then click on the **AutoCorrect Options** button.

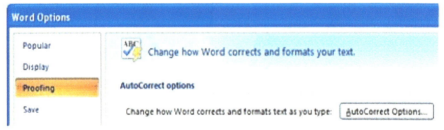

This will display the **AutoCorrect** dialog box.
· Click on the **AutoFormat As You Type** tab to see the **AutoCorrect** dialog box.

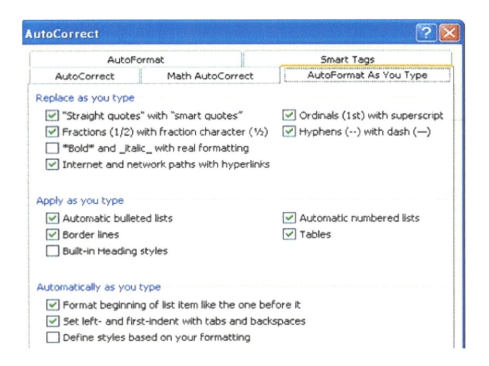

As you can see there are many formatting options that you can control, such as automatically applying **Smart quotes** rather than having the beginning and ending quotes that look the same.

Normal quotes look like this:

**'Normal Quotes'**

Smart Quotes look like this:

**'Smart Quotes'**

### Text Wrapping Options

You can control how text will 'flow' around a graphic. Type a document, save as **Text wrapping.** Close the document **Text wrapping**. Open the document called **Text**

**wrapping**. Click within the middle of the text, half way down the page. Click on the **Insert** tab and select **Picture**. Select and insert a picture into your document. Your document will look something like this one below:

**TEXT WRAPPING**

Text wrap is the behaviour of a near by graphic. One of me best ways to create visual impact in a publication is to wrap text around graphics
To Wrap Text around a Graphic
Select the graphic
• Choose Element menu – text wrap
• Click one of the wrap options

• Click OK
To wrap text around another text block, select the text block around which you want to wrap them choose Element–Group PageMaker now treats the text block like a graphic With the grouped text block selected, apply a text wrap option To wrap text around only three sides of a graphic, position either the left side or the right side (edge) of the graphic against a column guide
**There are two types of graphics in a PageMaker publication.**
1 **An Inline Graphic**, it behaves as part of a text in a publication Such a graphic is united to the text and moves along with that same text The graphic becomes stable within the text and can only be removed if transported to an independent graphic
2 **An Independent Graphic**, it is a graphic that does not behave as part of a text in a

If your picture is displayed much bigger than in the illustration, resize it so that it is smaller (by dragging one of the picture corners towards the centre of the picture).

As you can see the text does not flow around the picture. Right click on the picture and from the popup menu displayed, select the **Text.**

**Wrapping** command
From the submenu displayed, select a text wrapping option such as **Square**.

## TEXT WRAPPING

Text wrap is the behaviour of a near by graphic. One of me best ways to create visual impact in a publication is to wrap text around graphics

To Wrap Text around a Graphic

Select the graphic

• Choose Element menu – text wrap

• Click one of the wrap options

• Click OK

To wrap text around another text block around which you want to wrap then choose Element–Group PageM  text block like a graphic. With the grouped text block selected, apply a text  text around only three sides of a graphic, position either the left side or t  of the graphic against a column guide

**There are two types of graphics in a Pag**

1 **An Inline Graphic**; it behaves as part  Such a graphic is united to the text and moves along with that same tex  s stable within the text and can only be removed if transported to an indep

2 **An Independent Graphic**, it is a g  in a publication. Such a graphic is disunited wi

When you want a graphic to rem  phic
Any graphic that can be used as an independent graphic can also
Exceptions exist only with grouped objects

1 Choose Edit on the main menu bar and Click on Insert Object

2 A dialog box appears from which you can choose the progra  e g Microsoft Clip Gallery

3 Select the graphic you want and Click on Insert

You can resize the graphic to suit your choice and also p  own

Your text will now wrap around the picture, as illustrated below.

**TEXT WRAPPING**

Text wrap is the behaviour of a near by graphic. One of me best ways to create visual impact in a publication is to wrap text around graphics

To Wrap Text around a Graphic

Select the graphic

• Choose Element menu – text wrap

• Click  one of the wrap options

• Click OK

To wrap text around another text block, select the text block around which you want to wrap then choose Element–Group PageMaker now treats the text block like a graphic With the grouped text block selected, apply a text wrap option To wrap text around only three sides of a graphic, position either the left side or the right side (edge) of the graphic against a column guide

**There are two types of graphics in a PageMaker publication.**

1 **An Inline Graphic**; it behaves as part of a text in a publication Such a graphic is united to the text and moves along with that same text The graphic becomes stable within the text and can only be removed if transported to an independent graphic

2 **An Independent Graphic**, it is a graphic that does not behave as part of a text in a publication Such a graphic is disunited with the text

When you want a graphic to remain with a text, place the graphic as an inline graphic Any graphic that can be used as an independent graphic can also be used as an inline graphic Exceptions exist only with grouped objects

Experiment using some of the other text wrapping options: If you get lost remember that you can always use the **Undo** icon or Pres Ctrl+Z.

·* Save your changes and close the document.

**Animated Text Effects**

· Within Microsoft Word 2003 you could apply text animation effects to selected text. However there are no text animation effects within Microsoft Word 2007. If you have a document created using an earlier version of Microsoft Word you can still view text effects within Microsoft Word 2007.

· To remove text effects (created in a document using an earlier version of Microsoft Word), select that text from which you want to remove the animation effects and then press **Ctrl+Spacebar**.

## WordArt

· WordArt allows you to enter text and treat it as graphics within a document so that the text may be flipped, rotated, curved or subjected to other special effects. Once a WordArt object is inserted it may be enlarged or reduced using the normal drag and drop method for scaling graphics.

· Create a new document by pressing **Ctrl+N**. Type in your name, press the **Enter** key a few times to insert a few empty lines and save the document as **My WordArt**.

Click on the **Insert** tab and then click on the **WordArt** button.

The WordArt drop down list will be displayed, as illustrated.

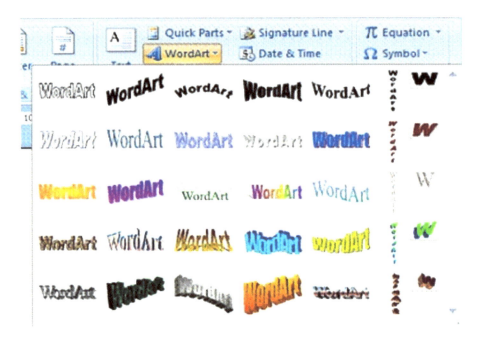

Click on a design that you like, and you will see the **Edit WordArt Text** dialog box.

Enter some text such as BRAVO. Click on the **OK** button and the name will be displayed using the design you selected.

You will notice when you select a WordArt object that WordArt specific controls are displayed, as illustrated.

· Click on some of the options within the **WordArt Styles** section to change the format.
· You can use the **Shadow Effect** control to add interesting shadow effects to your WordArt image.

· You can experiment with the **3-D** control to add interesting three dimensional effects.

If you have time investigate some of the other WordArt controls. If you get lost, you can use the **Undo** icon or Ctrl+Z to reverse your changes.

· Save your changes and close the file.

## Styling a Document for a Particular Purpose

Styles define the appearance of various text elements of your document such as headings, captions, and body text. When you apply a style to a paragraph or word, you can apply a whole group of character or paragraph formats or both in one simple operation. When you want to change the formatting of all the text of a particular element at once, you just change the style that is applied to that element. Styles make formatting your document easier. Additionally, they serve as building blocks for outlines and inserting of automatic tables of contents. When you use styles, you can change all text formatted with the style just by redefining the style.

· Type a document with first line 'Styles and Microsoft Word' and save as **Applying Styles**. Close the document.

· Open the document called **Applying Styles**. Click within the first line of text within the document, i.e. with the text:

**'Styles and Microsoft Word'**

· Click on the **Home** tab and select the required style from the **Styles** group. You can click on the **More** button to display additional style options.

174

*In this case select '**Heading 1**'

**Note**: To see how the style will look within a document, point to the style that you wish to preview, without actually clicking the mouse button.

· The first line of your document will now be formatted using the '**Heading 1**' style.

Click within one of the longer paragraphs within your document and experiment with applying different styles to that paragraph.

**Note**: To see more styles press **Ctrl+Shift+S** to open the **Apply Styles** task pane. Click on the **down arrow** within this control to display more style options, as illustrated. Experiment by applying some of these styles to paragraphs within your document.

· Save your changes and close the document.

**Modifying Styles**

· Microsoft Word is supplied with a number of available styles. You can easily modify an existing style. Open a document called **Modifying styles**. Select the first line and apply a '**Heading 1**' style to it. It should now look like this.

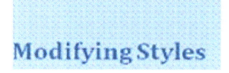

**Modifying Styles**

· We will now modify the '**Heading 1**' style so that it uses a different font and displays using a different colour.

Right click over the '**Heading 1**' quick style and from the popup menu displayed select the **Modify** command.

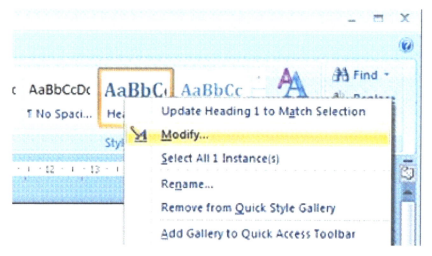

This will display the **Modify Style** dialog box.

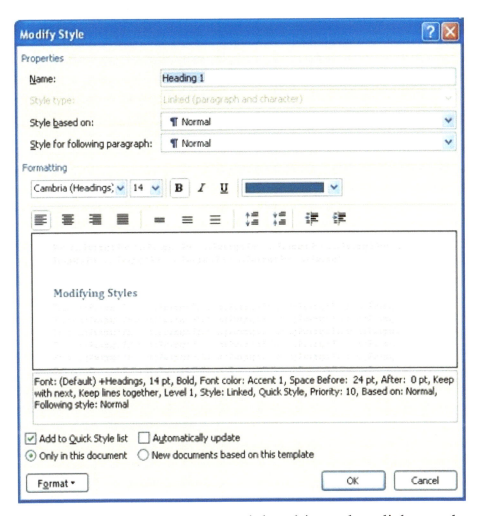

To change the font type used by this style, click on the **down arrow** next to the **Font** box, and select a different font, such as **Arial**.

· To change the font color used by this style click on the **down arrow** next to the **Font Color** box and select a different color, such as **Blue** or **Green**.

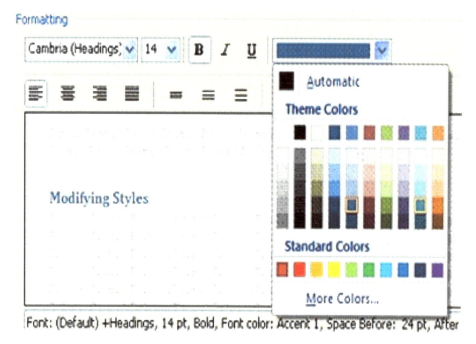

**Note**: If you look at the bottom of the dialog box, you will see details of how the modified style will be stored. If you select the '**Only in this document**' option then the style will only be modified within the active document. If however you wanted the modification to be available to all new documents that you subsequently create based on this template, then you would select the 'new documents based on this template' option. In this case make sure that '**Only in this document**' is selected.

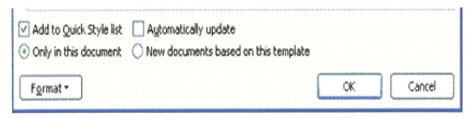

· Click on the **OK** button and the style will have been modified.

· Click on the header line lower down the page and apply the modified '**Header 1**' style to that paragraph.

· Save your changes and close the document.


**Creating Styles**

· Press **Ctrl+N** to create a new document. Type in *your name*. Press the **Enter** key a few times to insert a few empty lines. Select your text. Format your text using the **Arial** font, and to be displayed in **bold**, using a **20pt font size** and finally using a **red text colour**.

Press **Ctrl+Shift+S** to display the **Apply Styles** box. Type in the name of the new style, in this case **BigRed**, as illustrated.

Click on the **New** button and close the **Apply Styles** box.

· You can now type in some text at the bottom of your document and try applying the new style to that text.

· Save your changes and close the document.

**Using Outline View with Header Styles**

· Outline view displays the structure of a document. The indentations visible in Outline view provide an overview display of how your document is put together in terms of body text and header levels.

**Viewing a Document in Outline View**

· Type a document and Save as **Outline View**. Close the document. Open the document called **Outline View**.

Click on the **View** tab and then click on the **Outline** button.

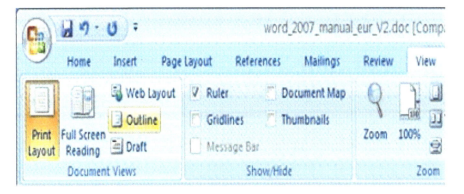

Your screen will now look like this.

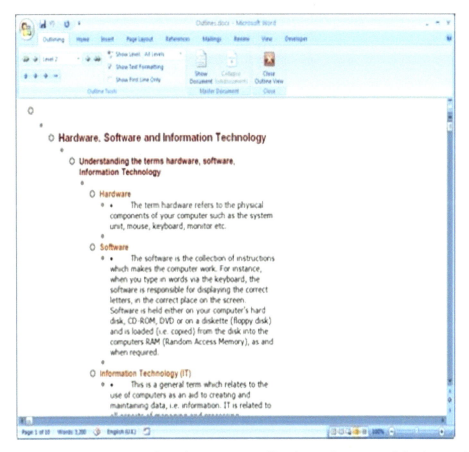

· As you can see the document displays layers of indented text. The indents relate to **Header 1**, **Header 2** levels etc and to body text within the document.

· Switch between **Print Layout** view and **Outline** view a few times as you move down the document. You should begin to see how the **Outline View** relates to the header structure within the document.

· Save any changes you have made and close the document.

**Creating a Document in Outline view**

· Create a new document by pressing **Ctrl+N**.

Click on the **View** tab and then click on the **Outline** button.

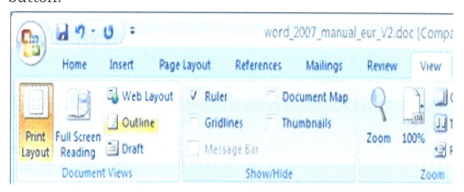

The **Outlining** ribbon will be displayed.

· Enter text for the first heading (anything will do) and press **Enter**. A first-level heading is inserted.

· To type another heading which is the same level as the previous heading, type in the new heading text and press **Enter**.

· To enter a heading that is a level below the previous heading (indented to its right), you demote the level heading. This is sometimes called a **subordinate** level. To demote a heading level, press **Tab**, or click the **Demote** icon (the right arrow) on the **Outlining** tab.

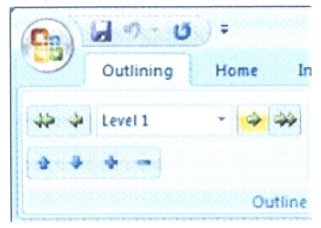

· To enter a heading that is a level above the previous heading (moved to its left), you promote the level heading. This is sometimes called a **superior** level. To promote a heading level, press **Shift-Tab**, or click the **Promote** icon (the left arrow) on the **Outlining** tab and then type the heading.

· To enter your body text after an outline heading, click on the **Demote to Body Text** button on the **Outlining** tab, or press **Alt+Shift+Right arrrow key**) and then type in the text.

**Note:**To use some of these keyboard shortcuts, ensure that the **Num Lock** is switched off.

· To move a heading up or down to a different location in the Outline, select the header you wish to move, click on the **Move Up** or **Move Down** button.

· To move a heading up or down to a different location in the Outline, select the header you wish to move, click on the **Move Up** or **Move Down** button.

· Experiment with entering different header levels into your document and every so often switch back to **Print Layout** view to see the effects of your work.

· Save your document as **My Outline Document**, and close the document.

**Templates**

· All documents that you create within Microsoft Word are based on templates. The default template is a file called

**Normal.dotm**. If you created a new document by pressing **Ctrl+N**, then you are not asked which template you want to use. A document is created based on information contained within the default template, i.e. **Normal.dotm**. Within this template formatting information is stored, such as the text size, font and colour. Much more formatting information such as margins, line spacing, etc is also stored within this file. If you wanted all new documents based on the default template to use a particular font, then all you would have to do is to modify the file, **Normal.dotm**.

· When you click on the **Office button**, and then click on the **New** command, you are offered a choice of templates on which to base the new document.

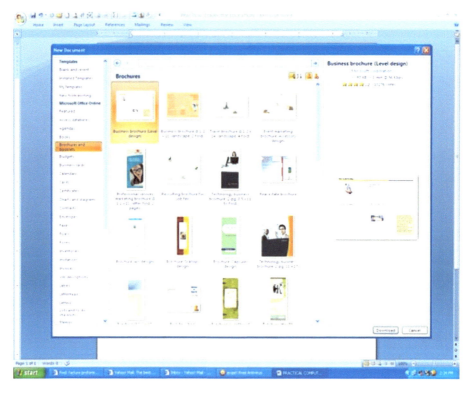

Each of these different options is stored in different templates. You can create your own template files and they will show up in the list of choices that you are offered within the new dialog box.

**Creating a New Template Based on an Existing Document or Template**

· You can create a template by creating a new document and then after customizing the document, save it as a template.

You can modify an existing document and save it as a template.

Lastly you can open an existing template and after making your modifications resave the template using a different name.

· As an example of creating a template, type a document and save as CAMERRON YOUTH AND VOCATIONAL EDUCATION. Close the document. Open the document called **CAMEROON YOUTH AND VOCATIONAL EDUCATION**. This is a document file, not a template file. Next to the text '**Name**' in the '**From**' section, type in your name. To save this document as a template, click on the **Office button** (top-left) and then click on the **Save As** command. Use the file name

Click on the **Trusted Templates** folder icon within the **Save As** dialog box.

· Click on the **down arrow** next to the **Save as type** section of the dialog box.  Select **Word Template**, as illustrated.

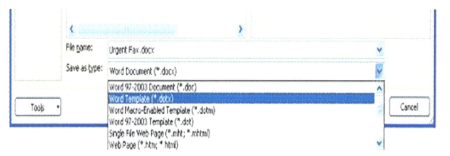

· Click on the **Save** button.

· Close the document.

To use this template, click on the **Office Button** and then click on the **New** command.

You will see the **New Document** dialog box similar to that illustrated below.

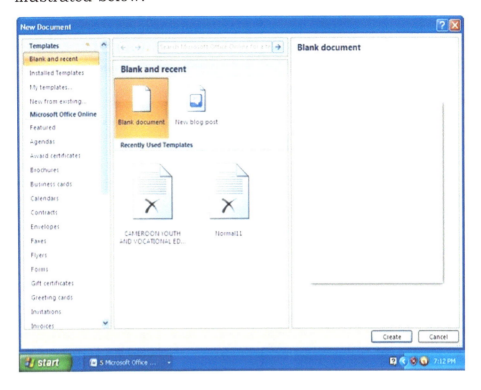

Click on the **My templates** option

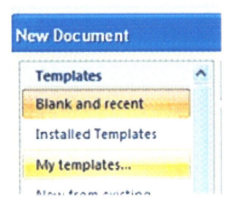

189

This will display the **New** dialog box. Select your template, in this case **CAMEROON YOUTH AND VOCATIONAL EDUCATION**, and click on the **OK** button.

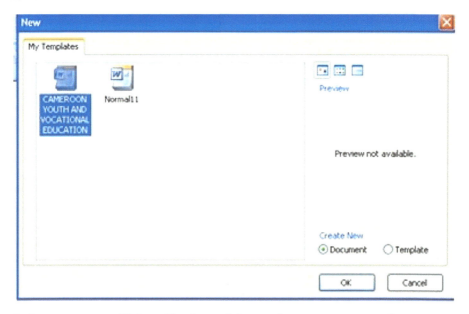

A document will be displayed based on your template.

**Note**: You have not opened the template file; you have created a new document based on the template. Any changes that you make to this new document will not affect the template file in any way.

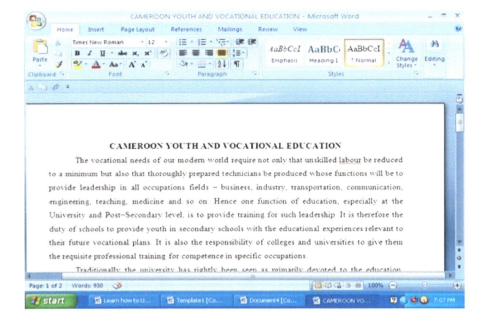

· Save the document as **Cameroon Youth and Vocational Education** and close the file.

**Customizing Normal.dotm**

· When you create a new document within Microsoft Word, by default the document is based on formatting information contained within a template file called **Normal.dotm**. If you open this template file and make any changes, then these changes will apply to all new documents that you create based on the default template.

· Opening the template file will vary slightly depending on whether you are using Windows XP or Windows Vista.

If you are using **Windows Vista**, then click on the **Microsoft Office Button**. From the menu displayed click on the **Open** command. Click on **Templates** and then double-click the **Normal.dotm** file to open it.

· If you are using **Windows XP**, then click on the **Microsoft Office Button**. From the menu displayed click on the **Open** command. Look in Trusted Templates and double click on the **Normal.dotm** file.

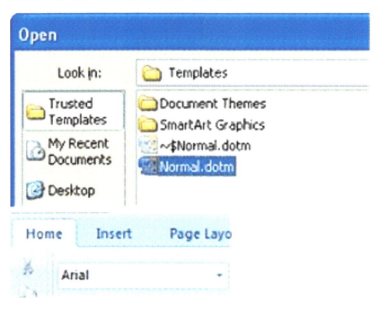

· When you have opened the template file, you should see the name **Normal** displayed within the Microsoft Word document title bar.

· You can make changes to this template now. Press **Ctrl+A** to select the entire (empty) document. Apply the **Arial** font (using the **Font** control on the **Home** tab).

· Make other changes such as increasing the margin sizes or setting the page layout to landscape (if you do not know how to do this try using the online **Help** available within Microsoft Word or refer page 67).

· Save your changes and close the template file.

· Create a new document based on the default template, by pressing **Ctrl+N**. Type in your name. You should find that the font used in this new document is the Arial font you specified in the Normal template file. Save the file as **My Arial Document**. Close the document.

## Sections and Columns

### Section Breaks

· Section breaks can be used to apply a particular layout or format to a page or range of pages, such as a chapter within a document. Using section breaks you could apply different chapter headers and footers to different chapters within a single document. Section breaks can be used to specify different formatting options for different parts of your document, including the following formatting and layout options:

| | |
|---|---|
| · Paper orientation | · Paper source when printing |
| ·  Page borders | · Vertical text alignment |
| · Headers and footers | · Columns |
| · Page numbering | · Line numbering |
| · Footnotes and endnotes | · Margins and Paper size |

### Creating Sections within a Document

· Type a document and save as **Sections**. Close the document called **Sections**.

· Open the document called **Sections**. Within the first page, click just in front of the text

### 'Section One'

Click on the **Page Layout** tab and then click on the **Breaks** button

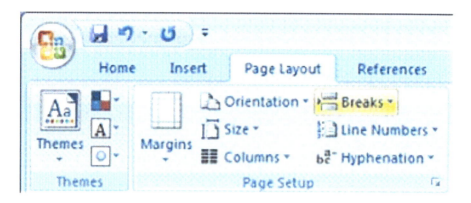

This will display the **Breaks** dialog box.

· As you can see you can insert **page breaks** within the top section of the dialog box and **section breaks** using the bottom section of the dialog box.

· There are different types of section breaks that you can insert into your document.

**Next Page**:

The new section will start on the next page within your document. The next page section break is often used for starting a new chapter within a document on a new page.

**Continuous**:

The new section starts on the same page. This type of section break is often used to control formatting such as displaying text within columns. When you format text as columns this type of section break is automatically setup up for you by Microsoft Word.

**Even Page**:

The new section starts on the next available even page within the document. This is often used for starting a new chapter within a document on an even page

**Odd Page**:

The new section starts on the next available odd page within the document. This is often used for starting a new chapter within a document on an odd page

· Select **Odd Page** section break from the dialog box. Click just in front of the text

'**Section two**'

and insert an odd section break.

**Note**: You would use the same method for even section breaks.

· View the document in **Print Preview** view. To do this click on the **Office button** (top-left of your screen), and then click on the **arrow** to the right of the **Print** command. From the menu displayed select the **Print Preview** command.

· Select the **Two Pages** option to make the effects of your formatting easier to view.

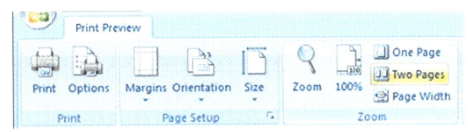

· Scroll up and down the document: as you can see each chapter starts on an odd page.

Click on the **Close Print View** command to return to the **Print Layout** view.

· Use the **Undo** icon to remove the section breaks you inserted and experiment with the effect of inserting the other types of section breaks into your document.

· Finally reinsert your odd page section breaks, save your changes and close the document.

## Viewing and Deleting Section Breaks within a Document

· As you have seen, you can manually insert section breaks within your document. However there are occasions when you will apply formatting to a document, such as column formatting where Microsoft Word will automatically insert section breaks for you. Type a document and save as **Mapoto Protocol**. Close the document **Mapoto Protocol.** Open thedocument called **Mapoto Protocol**. Select part of the first main paragraph, as illustrated.

The Protocol to the African Charter on Human and Peoples' Rights on the Rights of Women in Africa, better known as the Maputo Protocol, guarantees comprehensive rights to women including the right to take part in the political process, to social and political equality with men, to control of their reproductive health, and an end to female genital mutilation.[2] As the name suggests, it was adopted by the African Union in the form of a protocol to the African Charter on Human and Peoples' Rights.
Following on from recognition that women's rights were often marginalized in the context of human rights, a meeting organized by Women in Law and Development in Africa (WiLDAF) in March, 1995, in Lomé, Togo called for the development of a specific protocol to the African Charter on Human and People's Rights to address the rights of women. The OAU assembly mandated the African Commission on Human and Peoples' Rights (ACHPR) to develop such a protocol at its 31st Ordinary Session in June, 1995, in Addis Ababa.[3]

· Click on the **Page Layout** tab and click on the **Columns** button. From the drop down list displayed, select **Two**, to display the selected text as two column text.

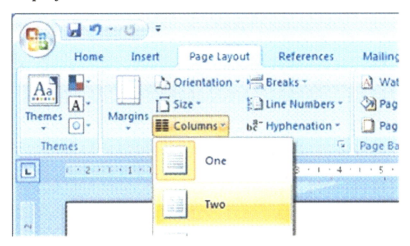

The document will now look like this.

The Protocol to the African Charter on Human and Peoples' Rights on the Rights of Women in Africa, better known as the Maputo Protocol, guarantees comprehensive rights to women including the right to take part in the political process, to social and political equality with men, to control of their reproductive health, and an end to female genital mutilation.[2] As the name suggests, it was adopted by the African Union in the form of a protocol to the African Charter on Human and Peoples' Rights.

Following on from recognition that women's rights were often marginalized in the context of human rights, a meeting organized by Women in Law and Development in Africa (WiLDAF) in March, 1995, in Lomé, Togo called for the development of a specific protocol to the African Charter on Human and People's Rights to address the rights of women. The OAU assembly mandated the African Commission on Human and Peoples' Rights (ACHPR) to develop such a protocol at its 31st Ordinary Session in June, 1995, in Addis Ababa.[5]

· You cannot see the section breaks in **Print Layout** view. Click on the **View** tab and select the **Draft** view from the **Document Views** section.

· You will be able to see the section break, as illustrated.

··············································Section Break (Continuous)·······································

· If you scroll down you will find another section break. The two column formatting is contained within the two section breaks.

· It is important to realize that a section break controls the section formatting of the text that precedes the section break.

· To illustrate this we will delete the first section break within your document. To do this, select the first section break and press the **Delete** key. Switch back to **Print Layout** view. You will see that the single column formatting of the first section within the document has been replaced by the two column formatting of the second section within the document. Click on the **Undo** icon to un-delete the first section break. Delete the second section break and then view the effect in **Print Layout** view. As you can see, this second section break contained the information about 2 columns formatting.

· Save your changes and close the document.

## Creating Multiple Column Layouts

· Type a document and save as **Columns**. Close the document. Open the document called **Columns,** and then click on the **Page Layout** tab. Click on the **Columns** command and you will see a drop down list of column formats.

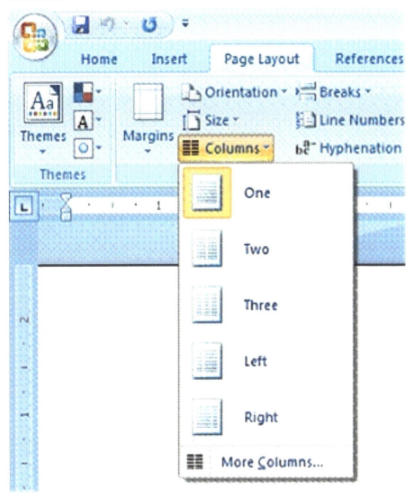

· Click on the **Two** column option and observe the effect. To more clearly see the effect, scroll to the start of the document and then click on the **View** tab and set the view to **Page Width**.

· Click on the **Page Layout** tab again and set the text to display as three columns.

·Experiment with using the **Left** and **Right** columns options (you may have to scroll to the first page to see the effect more clearly).

## Additional Column Formatting Options, Width and Spacing

· If necessary, click on the **Page Layout** tab and click on the **Columns** button. From the drop down menu displayed select the **More Columns** command. This will display the **More Columns** dialog box.

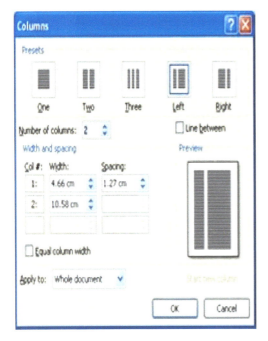

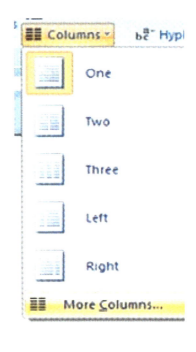

· You can use this dialog box to set column width and spacing. Experiment with setting exact width and spacing.

· Experiment with applying some of the other options within this dialog box, such as applying a vertically line between columns.

**Applying and Deleting Column Breaks**

· Format your document to display a two column layout. Display the first page on your screen. Approximately in the middle of the right column, click at the start of a sentence. We will insert a column break here so that everything after the point at which you clicked will be displayed in the next column. To do this click on the **Breaks** button (within the **Page Setup** section of the **Page Layout** tab). Select **Column**, as illustrated. Examine your document and you will see that the column break has shifted all subsequent text to the next column.

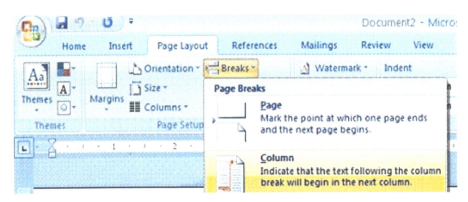

To remove a column break, you first need to be able to see exactly where the break has been inserted into a document. Click on the **Home** tab, and click on the **Show/Hide** icon. ¶

You will now be able to view any columns breaks within your document, as illustrated below.

> formatted·to·be·displayed·as·columns·within·your·document.·As·
> you·will·see·this·is·very·easy·to·do·within·Microsoft·Word.·This·is·
> text·that·will·be·formatted·to·be·displayed·as·columns·within·your·
> document.｜·················································· Column Break ··································

· To delete the column break, click on the column break and press **Delete** key.

· Save your changes and close the document.

**Tables within Microsoft Word**

· You can easily insert a table within your document. Each table is made up of individual cells. You can insert text or graphics in each cell. The cells or the entire table can be formatted using different borders and colour options.

**Creating a Table**

· Type a document and save as **Tabbed Text**. Close the document. Open the document called **Tabbed Text**. This document contains tabbed text which we will convert to a table format. To do this first select the tabbed text, as illustrated.

| Area | 2010 sales | 2011 sales |
|------|------------|------------|
| North West Region | 89 | 94 |
| South West Region | 57 | 98 |
| East Region | 64 | 83 |
| West Region | 23 | 77 |

Click on the **Table** option (within the **Insert** tab) and select the **Convert Text to Table** option, which will display the **Convert Text to Table** dialog box.

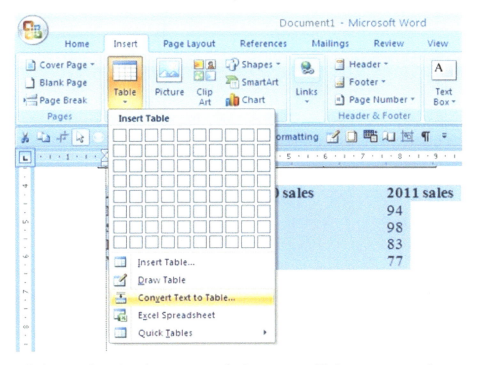

Click on the **OK** button and the text will be converted to a table format, as illustrated.

| Area | 2010 sales | 2011 sales |
|---|---|---|
| North West Region | 89 | 94 |
| South West Region | 67 | 98 |
| East Region | 64 | 83 |
| West Region | 23 | 77 |

· Save your changes and close the document

**Sorting Data within a Table**

Type a document which contains a small table and save as **Table Manipulation**. Close the document. Open the document called **Table Manipulation**, which contains a small table. Click within the second column and then click on the **Sort** icon (within the **Home** tab). This will display the **Sort** dialog box

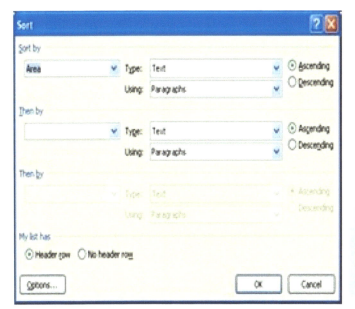

· You can select **Ascending** or **Descending** options. Try clicking on the **Ascending** button and click on the **OK** button. Observe the effect on your table. Try ordering the column in **Descending** order. Click within the final column and experiment with sorting this in ascending and then descending order.

If you look closely at the **Sort** dialog box, you will see there is an option to set the first row as a header row. This means that when you sort the data within the column, the top header row is not included within the sort and still remains as the top row after the sort. The presence of a header row is normally picked up automatically by Microsoft Word.

You will also notice that there is a **Sort by Type** option allowing you to sort using **Text**, **Number** or **Date**.

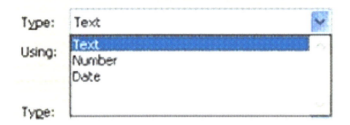

Save your changes and close the document.

**Formulas and Tables**

· Type a document which contains a table and save as **Table Sums.** Close the document. Open the document called **Table Sums**.

· Click within the empty cell next to the word **Totals**.

Click on the **Layout** tab and then click on the **Formula** command (located within the **Data** section of the **Layout** tab).

This will display the **Formula** dialog box.

206

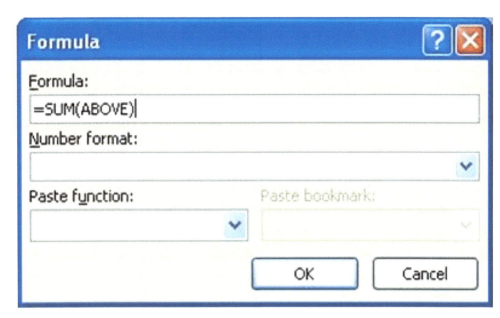

By default the **Sum** formula is displayed which will sum up all the numbers in the column above the cell you clicked in. Click on the **OK** button and the numbers in the column will be added up automatically.

| | |
|---|---:|
| North West Region | 1854 |
| South West Region | 2874 |
| East Region | 7723 |
| West Region | 8837 |
| **Totals** | **21288** |

· Change the figures relating to the **North West Region** from **1854** to **644**. You may notice that the total value at the bottom of the columns does not change.

| | |
|---|---:|
| North West Region | 644 |
| South West Region | 2874 |
| East Region | 7723 |
| West Region | 8837 |
| **Totals** | **21288** |

207

· Click on the cell containing the total value and press the **F9** update key. The total is now updated.

| | |
|---|---:|
| North West Region | 644 |
| South West Region | 2874 |
| East Region | 7723 |
| West Region | 8837 |
| **Totals** | **20078** |

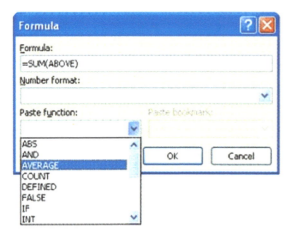

Click on the cell containing the total. Click on the **Formula** button again. Click on the **down arrow** within the **Paste function** section of the dialog box. As you can see there are other functions available, such as **Average, Count, IF** etc. Do same with other functions.

· Save your changes and close the document.

**Merging and Splitting Cells within a Table**

· A table is made up of individual cells. You can easily select multiple cells and merge them so that they act as a single cell. You can also split a cell into two or more cells.

· Type the table below and save it as **Cells.** Close the document.

Open the document called **Cells**.

**Merging Cells**

· Within the upper table, click within cell **3**. Press the mouse button and while keeping it pressed down, drag the mouse pointer down so that cell **6** is also selected. Release the mouse button. Cells **3** and **6** are now selected.

| 1 | 3 | 4 |
|---|---|---|
| 5 | 6 | 7 |
| 8 | 9 |  |

* Right click over the selected cells and from the popup menu displayed select the **Merge Cells** command.

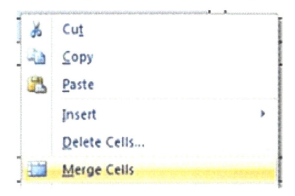

·The table will now look like this.

| 1 | 3 | 4 |
|---|---|---|
| 5 | 6 | 7 |
| 8 | 9 |  |
|  | 10 |  |

· Select cells **9** and **10**. Merge these cells so that the table now looks like this.

| | | |
|---|---|---|
| 1 | 3 6 | 4 |
| 5 | | 7 |
| 8 | 9 10 | |
| | | |

## Splitting Cells

· Within the lower table, select cells **6** and **9**.

| | | |
|---|---|---|
| 1 | 3 | 4 |
| 5 | 6 | 7 |
| 8 | 9 | 10 |

Click on the **Layout** tab and click on the **Split Cells** button.

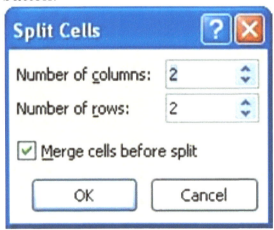

This will display the **Split Cells** dialog box.

· Click on the **OK** button. Your table should now look like this.

| 1 | | 3 | 4 |
|---|---|---|---|
| 5 | 6 | 9 | 7 |
| 8 | | | 10 |

· Save your changes and close the document.

## Graphics within Microsoft Word 2007

· There are a variety of graphic formats that you can insert into your Microsoft Word document.  Under the **Insert** tab, you will see the following options.

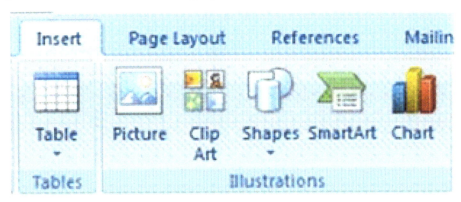

## Inserting Shapes

Create a new document and save as **Shapes**. Close the document. Open the document called **Shapes**.  Click on the **Insert** tab and click on the **Shapes** option.

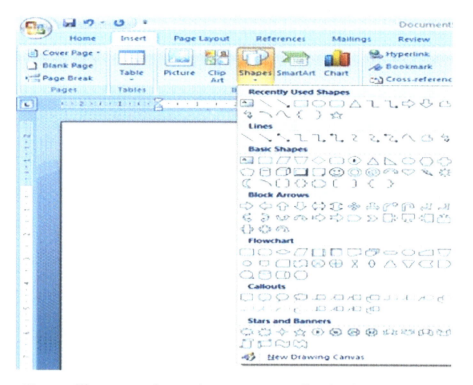

· You will see a drop down menu displaying a range of shapes. Try inserting the '**Smiley Face**' shape, as illustrated.

· Once you click on a shape, you will see that the mouse pointer changes to a cross-hair shape. Move the pointer over the document and depress the mouse button, and while keeping the mouse button depressed, move the mouse pointer diagonally down the page. When you let go of the mouse button the shape will be displayed within your document.

**Note**: The smiley face may appear more oval than circular. Select the shape and delete the shape. Insert the same shape again, but this time, hold down the **Shift** key while you drag the mouse pointer diagonally down the page. When you release the mouse button you will see that the shape is perfectly circular. This technique can also be used to produce square shapes, as opposed to oblong shapes.

· Insert a triangle and rectangle shape, so that the document now contains three shapes.

· To move your shapes within the document, click on the shape to highlight it and then press the mouse button down and while keeping it pressed down, drag the shape from one place to another.

· Drag the shapes so that they slightly overlap each other, as illustrated.

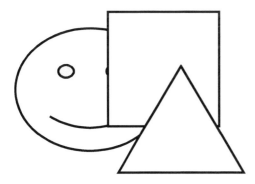

**Reordering Graphics**

· In the example shown, the triangle is at the bottom of the heap. The smiley face is in the middle and the rectangle is at the top. You can rearrange this layering. Click on the top shape to select it and then right click over the selected shape. You will see a popup menu as illustrated.

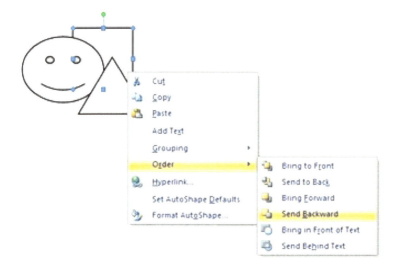

· Select the **Send to Back** command and you will see the following.

· Experiment with sending different shapes to the back and also bring objects at the back to the front.

· In this case where there are three layers of objects you can also use the **Bring Forward** or **Send Backward** commands. These commands can be used to bring an object at the back up to the middle layer, or move an object at the top down to the middle layer. Experiment with moving objects up or down one layer at a time. Save your changes and close the document.

**Placing a Picture or Graphic In front or Behind text**

· You can also place a **picture or graphic** in front of text or behind text. Type a document containing any pyramid and save as **pyramidal hut**.Close the document. Open the document called **pyramidal hut** or equivalence.

The picture is displayed on top of the text by default.

To display the picture behind the text, right click on the pyramidal picture or graphic and from the popup menu select the **Send Behind Text** command.

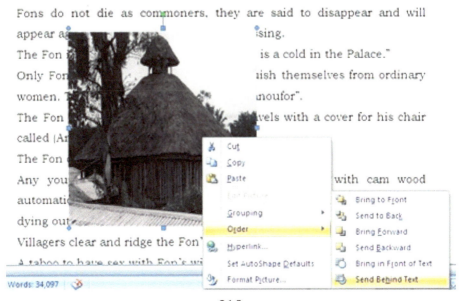

- Fons do not die as commoners, they are said to disappear and will appear again. Tradition says the Fon is missing.
- The Fon is never sick, tradition says "there is a cold in the Palace."
- Only Fons wives wear cowries to distinguish themselves from ordinary women. The Fon's drinking cup is called "anoufor".
- The Fon does not sit on a bare sit. He travels with a cover for his chair called (Ar......
- The Fon c.......
- Any young ........ed with cam wood automatical..... dying out because of human .....
- Villagers clear and ridge the .....
- A taboo to have sex with Fon'....

· You may be wondering how to select an object that is displayed behind the text. To do this display the **Home** tab. Click on the **Select** button and you will see a drop down menu.

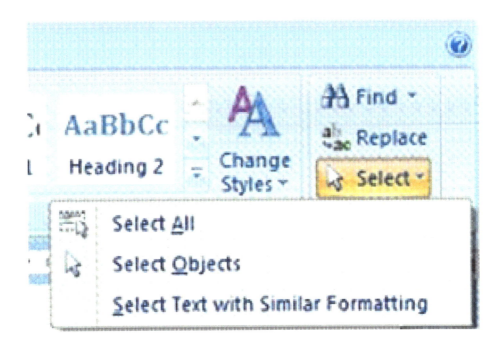

· Select the **Select Objects** command. You can now click on objects displayed behind the text. Right click on the object displayed behind the text and you will see a popup menu. To reset the shape to display in front of the text, click on the **Bring in Front of Text** command.

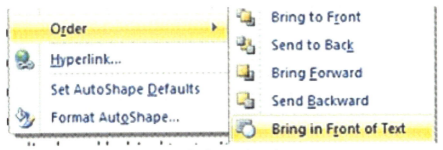

· Save your changes and close the document.

**Modifying Image Colours and Borders**

· Create a new document and insert a **rectangle** shape. You can use the **Shape Style** options to add colours to your shapes. Click on the coloured square to apply the colour to the shape.

· Click on the **down arrow** to the right of the **Shape Style** options to display a drop down with more colour options. You can click on the **Shape Fill** icon to display more fill options. Experiment with these to modify the fill **Gradient**, **Texture** and **Pattern**. To remove these effect use the **No Fill** option.

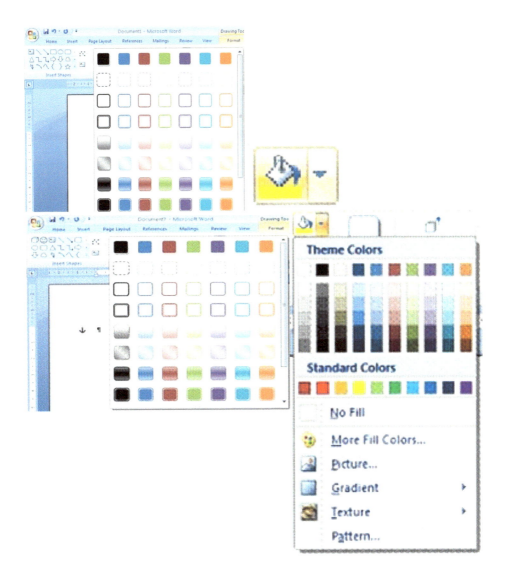

You can click on the **Shape Outline** icon to display more outline options.

· Click on the **Weight** command and you will be able to adjust the thickness of the shape border. Experiment.

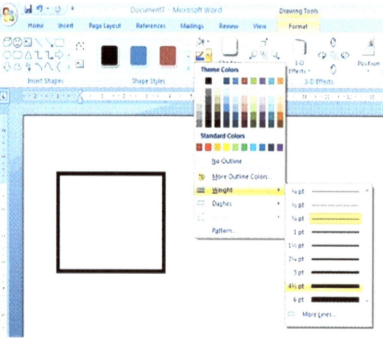

Select the **Dashes** command to use a border made up of dashes. Experiment.

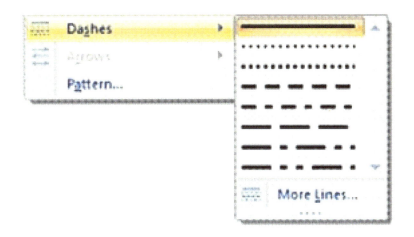

· Save your changes and close the document.

**Grouping or Ungrouping Pictures**

·Type a document and import three pictures into it. Save as **Pictures**. Close the document. Open the document called **Pictures**. This document contains three separate pictures. Each picture can be moved and formatted independently to the other pictures. We can group these individual pictures so that they act as a single shape. Select each picture one at a time to demonstrate that there are indeed three separate pictures within the document.

Now we need to select all the pictures so that we can group them into a single picture. To do this click on the first picture to select it. While keeping the **Ctrl** key depressed click on the other two pictures. When you release the **Ctrl** key the three pictures will remain selected, as illustrated.

· Right click over the selected shapes and from the popup menu displayed select the **Grouping** command. From the submenu select the **Group** command.

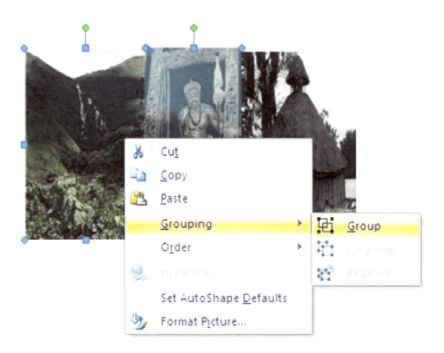

222

The three pictures now act as a single object, as illustrated below.

Try applying gray scale to the pictures and you will see that it is applied to all three grouped objects, as illustrated below.

· Save your changes and close the document.

**Inserting a Watermark**

· Type the birth certificate below and save as **Birth Certificate**. Close the document. Open the document called **Birth Certificate**. Click on the **Page Layout** tab and click on the **Watermark** button. From the drop down menu displayed select the **Custom Watermark** command.

· This will display the **Picture Watermark** dialog box. You can insert either text or picture watermarks.

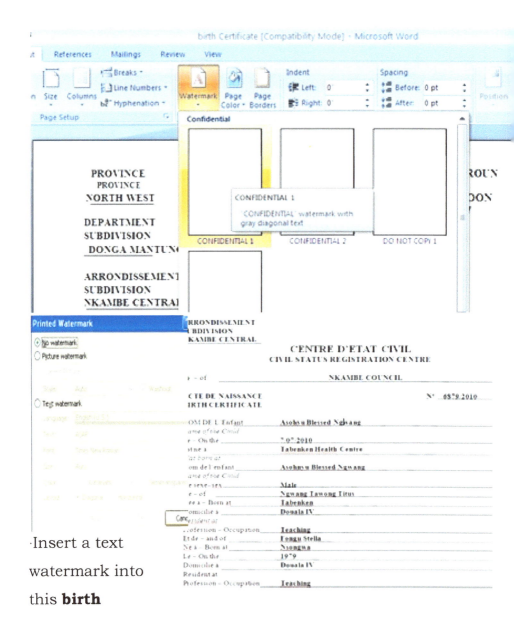

·Insert a text watermark into this **birth**

**certificate**. To do this, click on the **Text watermark** button. You can type in custom text or in this case click on the **down arrow** to the right of the **Text** section and select **DO NOT COPY**. You can also experiment with selecting different fonts and colours. Leave the **Semitransparent** option checked and leave the size set to **Auto**. Normally it will display the watermark diagonally. When you have finished, click on the **OK** button to see the effect. If you selected a very light watermark colour you may find it hard to see. If you select a very dark watermark colour you may find it hard to read the text in front of the watermark. Experiment to find a good colour balance. The birth certificate is as shown above.

· Save your changes and close the document.

· Open again the document called **birth certificate** which contains a few lines of text. Click on the **Page Layout** tab and click on the **Watermark** button. From the drop down menu displayed select the **Custom Watermark** command. This time select the **Picture Watermark** option.

· Click on the **Select Picture** button. Navigate to the folder containing your picture files and select a picture file called for example **Trainees Tobby Vision Computers**. Click on the **Insert** button and you will return to the **Printed Watermark** dialog box.

Uncheck the **Washout** option and click on the **OK** button.

## CENTRE D'ETAT CIVIL
### CIVIL STATUS REGISTRATION CENTRE

de – of _____ NKAMBE COUNCIL _____

**ACTE DE NAISSANCE**                                      N° _6879/2010_
**BIRTH CERTIFICATE**

NOM DE L'Enfant _____ **Asohvu Blessed Ngwang** _____
*Name of the Child*
Le – On the _____ **7/07/2010** _____
Est né à _____ **Tabenken Health Centre** _____
*Was born at*
Nom de l'enfant _____ **Asohvu Blessed Ngwang** _____
*Name of the Child*
De sexe–sex _____ **Male** _____
De – of _____ **Ngwang Tawong Titus** _____
Nee a – Born at _____ **Tabenken** _____
Domicilié à _____ **Douala IV** _____
*Résident at*
Profession – Occupation _____ **Teaching** _____
Et de – and of _____ **Fongu Stella** _____
Ne à – Born at _____ **Nsongwa** _____
Le – On the _____ **1979** _____
Domicilié à _____ **Douala IV** _____
Resident at
Profession – Occupation _____ **Teaching** _____

- Save your changes and close the document.

## *Text Boxes*

· Text boxes allow you to create areas on the screen into which you can place text or graphics, which can be formatted independently of the main body of text within a document.

## Inserting a Text Box

Creat a doument save as **Text Box.** Close the **Text Box** document.

Open the document called **Text Box**. Click on the **Insert** tab and click on the **Text Box** option (displayed within the **Text** section of the **Insert** tab). This will display a drop down menu as illustrated.

· Click on the **Draw Text Box** command. When you move the mouse pointer over the text within your document you will notice that the pointer has changed to a crosshair shape. Click at the location within your document that you want to insert the Text Box. The Text Box will be inserted as illustrated.

**DEFINITION OF EDUCATION**

It would for example be a serious misunderstanding if it were assumed that African attention was fixed exclusively on the formal education associated with institutions and the classroom on questions of curricula, time-tables, certificates, examinations, pedagogical gadgets and tricks of the trade. [...] rvey the Western Group devotes a chapter to what it likes to call "informal E[...] tem Group gives about a tenth of its sections to what it prefers to call "Adult[...] Conference itself one of its five subdivisions is wholly concerned with [Edu...] dult] There can be few educational surveys which give the diffusion of education so integral a place in its thinking and policy

It was indeed from Africa that the original impetus towards "Mass Education" derived The Colonial Office Report published under that title in 1944 was related to African experience

## Resizing, Moving and Deleting a Text Box

· You can use the handles around the edge of the Text Box to resize the Text Box. Try this now, by clicking on one of the handles (located at each corner or half way along each edge), and while keeping the mouse button depressed drag the edge to a new location giving you a large or smaller box depending on the direction you drag. When you release the mouse button you will see the resized Text Box displayed within your document.

To move the Text Box click on the edge of the text (be sure not to click on a **handle** object along the edge or at each corner). The mouse pointer will change to a shape containing four arrows all pointing outwards. While keeping the mouse button pressed move the mouse so that the Text Box is dragged to the new location. When you release the mouse button, you will see the Text Box displayed at the next location.

· To delete a Text Box, click on the edge of the text (be sure not to click on a handle object along the edge or at each corner). The Text Box is now selected and when you press the **Delete** key the Text Box will be deleted.

· Click on the **Undo** icon to reverse deleting the text box.

**Inserting Text or a Graphic into a Text Box**

· Resize your Text Box so that you can enter a few lines of text. Type your name into the Text Box. You can edit the text in the Text Box in exactly that same way that you edit text within the body of your document. Delete your name. Type in the days of the week. Experiment with formatting each day using a different font type. Apply **bold** and **italic** formatting to some of the day names.

· Save your changes and close the file.

## Formatting Text Boxes with Border and Shading Effects

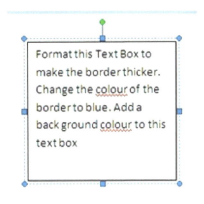

· Open a document called **Text Box Formatting**. Click on the text border to select the Text Box, as illustrated below.

· You should see Text Box options, as illustrated

**Note**: If you do not see these options double click on the **Text Box border**.

To change the Text Box border thickness, click on the **Shape Outline** button to display a drop down menu. Click on the **Weight** command and then select the required border thickness. Experiment with applying different border thicknesses. Selecting **No Outline** will remove the border display from the Text Box. Experiment again.

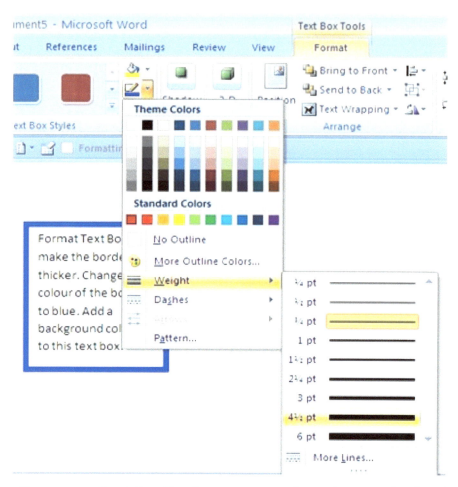

. You can select the **Dashes** command to change the border style.

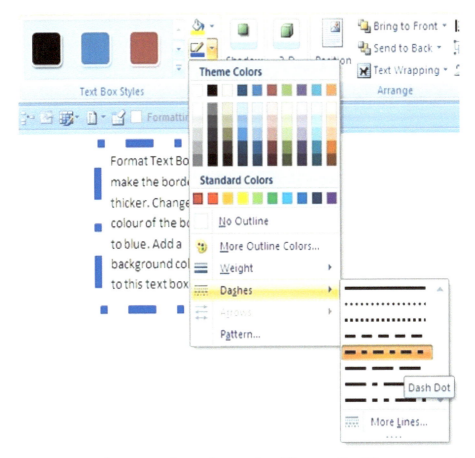

You can select a colour from the **Shape Outline** menu to change the colour of the border.

· To set a background colour for a Text Box, select one of the colours displayed, and click on the **down arrow** to the right of these colour choices to reveal more colours options.

· Save your changes and close the document.

**Linking Text Boxes**

· Create a document and save
as **Text Box.**

· Close the document **Text Box.**

· Open a document called **Text
Box Linking**.

· Start to type a short sentence
into the first Text Box and stop when you can no longer see
what you are typing in. As you can clearly see, by default
text does not flow from one Text Box to another. ·

· Double click on the Text Box **border** to display Text Box
related options in the Ribbon. Click on the **Create Link**

button. Move the mouse pointer over the second Text Box and click. This will link the two Text Boxes and the text will now flow from the first Text Box to the second Text Box. If you wish to remove this link you can use the **Break Link** command.

Save your changes and close the document

## What is Mail Merging?

The Mail Merge feature is used to insert variable data into a fixed format by combining two files into one file. Two files need to be created before you can merge them; these are the data file and the main document file. The variable information, such as names and addresses, is stored in the data file ready to merge into the main document file. The information, which remains constant and the field names are stored in the main document file, where each field name relates to a field name in the data file. The data in the two files is merged as a series of personalized letters or envelopes.

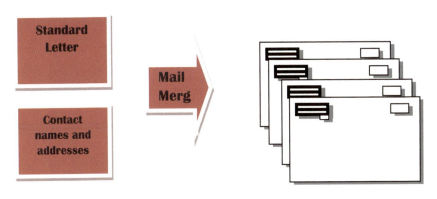

## Starting the Mail Merge Wizard

· Create a document and save as **Interview Schedule**. Close the document **Interview Schedule**. Open the document called **Interview Schedule**. This is typical of a general letter which can be individually addressed and mailed. In order to mail merge this letter we need to insert codes to tell Microsoft Word where to insert items such as the name and address of each person we are going to send this letter to. We also need to tell Microsoft Word which list of names and addresses we are going to use and where this list is stored.

· To start the process, click on the **Mailings** tab. Click on the **Start Mail Merge** button.

## Mail Merge Wizard - Step 1 of 6 'Select document type'

· From the drop down list displayed, select the **Step by Step Mail Merge Wizard** command.

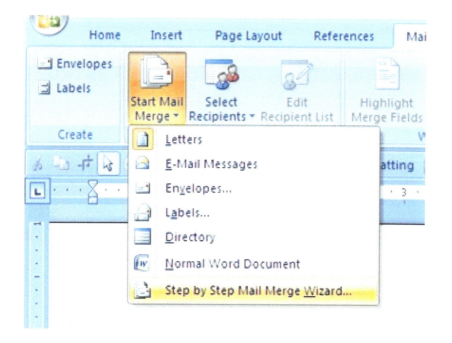

You will see a panel displayed to the right of your document. In this case we wish to produce a mail merged letter, so we will use the **Letters** selection.

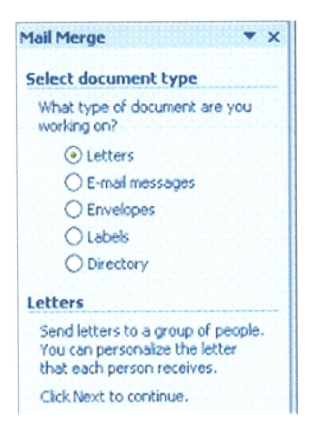

· At the bottom right of the screen you have the option of clicking on '**Next: Starting document**' to take you to the next page of the mail merge wizard.

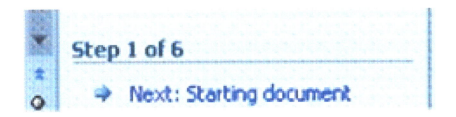

· **Mail Merge Wizard - Step 2 of 6 'Select Starting document'**

· You will see the following options displayed to the right of your document. In this case we will use the current document that is displayed on your screen.

Click on **Next** at the bottom right of your screen.

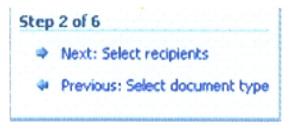

· **Mail Merge Wizard - Step 3 of 6 'Select recipients'**
· The next step of the wizard lets you determine which list of recipients will be used for the mail merge process.

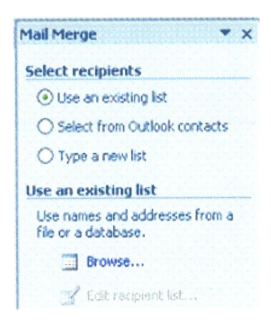

In this case we will select the option **Use an existing list**.

· Click on the **Browse** button. This will display the **Select Data Source** dialog box.

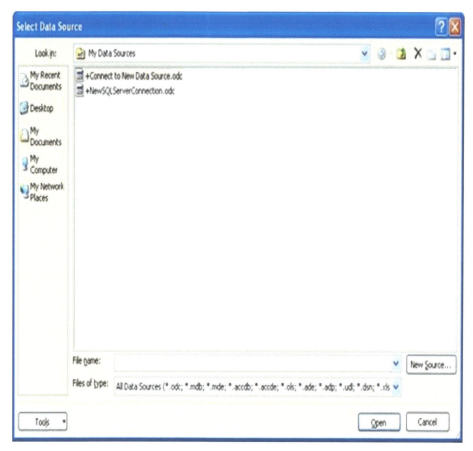

· Use this dialog box to navigate to the folder containing a list called **ENS BAMBILI**. Select this file.

· Click on the **Open** button. This will display the **Select Table** dialog box because I have produced the list in MS Excel.

Click on the **OK** button which will display the **Mail Merge** · **Recipients** dialog box.

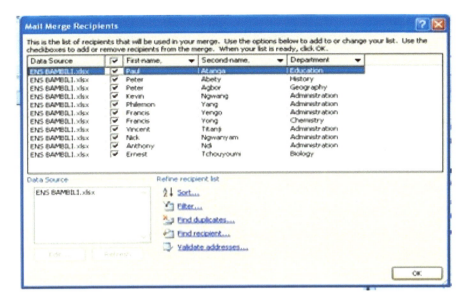

· Click on the **OK** button to continue.

Click on the **Next** option at the bottom right of the screen.

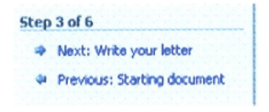

· **Mail Merge Wizard - Step 4 of 6 'Write your letter'**

The following options are displayed to the right of your

document.

· Click at the start of your document (where we insert the codes relating to the person to whom the letter is addressed).

· Click on **More items**.

This will display the **Insert Merge Field** dialog box.

· Click on the **More items** command. This will display the **Insert Merge Field** dialog box.

· Make sure that **First name** is selected and then click on the **Insert** button. Click on the **Close** button. Press the **Space bar**.

· Click on the **More items** command. This will display the **Insert Merge Field** dialog box.

· Make sure that **Last name** is selected and then click on the **Insert** button. Click on the **Close** button. Press the **Enter** key.

· Click on the **More items** command. This will display the **Insert Merge Field** dialog box.

Make sure that **Department** is selected and then click on the **Insert** button. Click on the **Close** button.

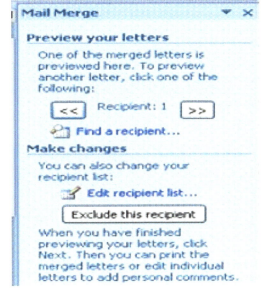

Your document should now contain the following merge field codes.

«FirstName» «LastName»

«Department»

**Mail Merge Wizard - Step 5 of 6 'Preview your letters'**

The following options are displayed to the right of your document

· Click on the **Next** option at the bottom right of the screen.

**Mail Merge Wizard - Step 6 of 6**

· This is the final stage of the Mail Merge Wizard. You will see the following choices.

If you were to click on the **Print** option, you would see the **Merge to Printer** dialog box which lets you select what to print.

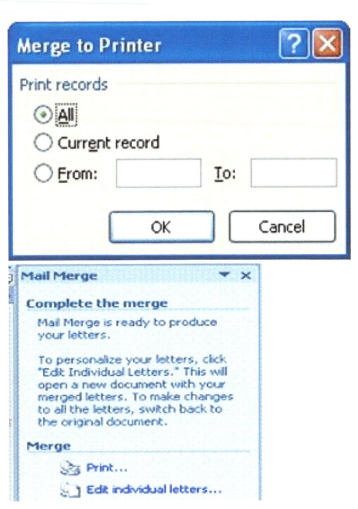

· In this case click on the **Edit Individual letters** option. You will see the following dialog box which lets you select what to merge.

· Click on the **OK** button to merge all the print records. A new document will be created containing your mail merged letters. In real life you could check through this and print later. In this case to save paper we will not actually print this document. Scroll through the document to see if everything is as you expected. Save the document as **My First Mail Merge**. Close the mail merged document.

· Close the open document and save your changes.

**Microsoft Word Shortcut keys**

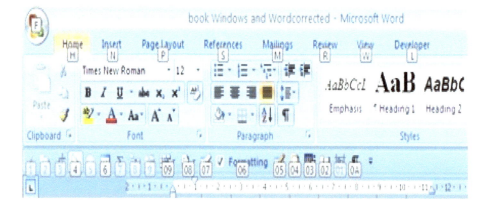

## Viewing Shortcuts

Some shortcuts contain more characters to be pressed on the keyboard. Use Office Help (F1) and type **Keyboard shortcuts for Microsoft Office Word** to browse and master the keyboard shortcuts as shown below.

If you like using shortcut keys instead of the mouse, you need to know that they work a bit differently in Office 2007 compared to previous versions. Using shortcut keys is often easier than the mouse. Shortcut keys are combinations of keyboard keystrokes that give you access to most of the functions you would otherwise select using the mouse.

By pressing the Alt key on your keyboard some small boxes with numbers or letters will be displayed above the Quick Access Toolbar, Office Button and the individual Tabs in the Ribbon. The numbers and letters that appear correspond to the key you should press to select the function. For this you no longer need to press the Alt key simultaneously. For example, if you press "N", the Insert Tab is displayed, and the features in this Tab will be automatically highlighted with shortcuts. All you need to do is press what is in the small boxes without pressing the Alt key (see screen shot viewing shortcut keys page 146).

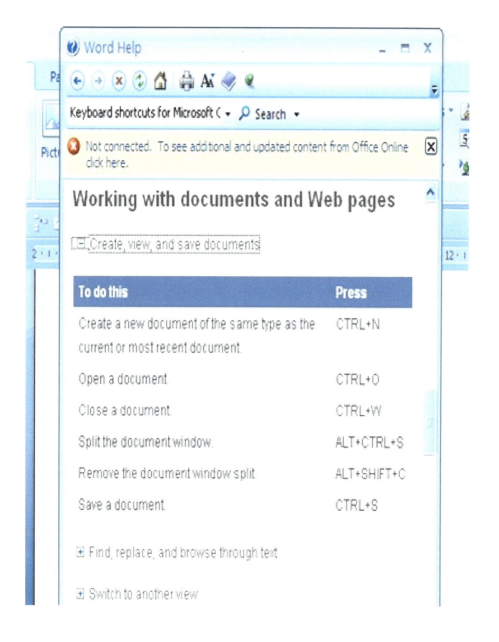

**Working with documents and Web pages**

⊟ Create, view, and save documents

| To do this | Press |
|---|---|
| Create a new document of the same type as the current or most recent document. | CTRL+N |
| Open a document. | CTRL+O |
| Close a document. | CTRL+W |
| Split the document window. | ALT+CTRL+S |
| Remove the document window split. | ALT+SHIFT+C |
| Save a document. | CTRL+S |

⊞ Find, replace, and browse through text

⊞ Switch to another view

# INTERNET

## What is the Internet?

Internet, also called the Net, is a global collection of computers connected to each other. This global network links thousands of computers at universities, research institutions, government agencies and business houses throughout the world. Using a small PC at your home and a telephone connection, you can reach anywhere in the world through the Internet. You can access information on thousands of topics ranging from designing toys to making atomic bombs. Each computer connected to the Internet can communicate with other computers. Messages or information sent or received on the Internet is in the form of files. Information travels over the Internet via a variety of languages known as protocols. In Internet, computers communicate with each other through the Transmission Control Protocol/Internet Protocol (TCP/IP).

## Things you can do on the Internet

## Email – Your New Postman

Electronic mail or email is the most widely used feature of the Internet. It has now become a vital tool of communication for people. Email has not only impressed technocrats but also caught the fancy of all – be it a school kid, a housewife or a business tycoon. Many internet users use it for emailing only. This service has enabled millions of Internet users all over the world to send and receive written messages in a few seconds. Email is basically a file that is sent from one computer to another through a network. In the 1970s Email was just about sending text messages but today you can send different types of files such as scanned/faxed images, computer graphics or sound and video files along with your email messages.

**Advantages of Email**

· It saves lot of paper and the chance of email getting misplaced is almost nil.

· Messages can be transmitted in a few seconds.

· Messages can be sent at any time of the day as per sender's convenience.

· Copies of a single email can be sent to multiple users.

· Both incoming and outgoing messages can be saved for future reference.

**Chatting**

The chatting feature of the Internet lets you instantly communicate with people anywhere in the world by sending and receiving messages in real time. Using Internet Relay Chat (IRC) you can also converse on the Net with more than one individual simultaneously. IRC is a chat protocol that uses the Internet to exchange text messages among users. Chat room is the hub of Internet chatting. A chat room is actually a computer (chat server) that allows many persons to log on at the same time. When you enter a chat room, you see the names of people who are already there, and a window in which a few lines of text are constantly moving upwards. These lines are the messages being sent by various members of the chat room to their chat partners. Once you join a room, you can read other person's messages and then send your messages to one or all the chatters. Every chatter has a log in name, which he uses for his identification, and whatever is typed appears in the general conversation window. However, if you want to chat with only one chatter, you and that person can enter a private room to have a private conversation. Broadly, there are two categories of chatting, discussed here under.

i.) Text–based chat: It is the oldest, the simplest and the most popular mode of chat on the Internet. This mode enables you to communicate, through messages, with one or more persons. During chatting when you type text in the message window, the text appears on the computer screen of every person participating in your conversation (that is, the individuals that are there in the message window).

ii.) e-based or Multimedia Chat: In this type of conversation, you make use of multimedia. e-based chat enables you to have voice conversations with your friends through live video over the Internet. Since sound and video signals get transferred slowly across the Internet, it is recommended that you use a high-speed modem for e-based chat.

**Search Engines**

Search engine is software that searches a particular piece of information according to the specified criteria. You can just log on to any search engine and get the required information without much effort and wastage of time. Some popular search engines are Google, Yahoo, MSN, Alta Vista, Look Smart, Netscape and Info space.

**Educate yourself with e–Learning**

Electronic Learning (e–Learning) is the mode of acquiring knowledge by means of the Internet, and computer based training programs. In this type of education, students study on their own at home or office and communicate with the faculty and other students via email, electronic forums, video conferencing, chat rooms, bulletin boards, instant messaging and other forms of computer–based communication.

**e–Commerce –** Way of doing business on the Internet. The concept of e–Commerce is similar to Commerce, which means exchange of goods and services for their worth. Conversely, e–Commerce differs from commerce in that it involves selling and purchasing of commodities and services using a computer network, usually the Internet. The main elements of e–Commerce are listed below:

· Product: To conduct e–Commerce, you must have some product to sell.

· Selling place: In e–Commerce, the place of selling and ordering goods is a website.

· Accessibility to people: This element decides how people would access the website that is hosting e–Commerce.

· How to place orders: The website must have some online forms that people can use to place their orders.

· How to accept money from customers: In e–Commerce, credit card is the most convenient and commonly used means of accepting money from customers.

· Delivery mechanism: The website that is hosting e–Commerce must have the provision to deliver commodities to their customers. If the nature of the commodity is such that it can be delivered online, like some music, e–book, images etc., and then delivery could be made online, otherwise the website must deliver the commodity manually at the customer's doorstep.

**Surfing the Internet**

When you hear people talking about surfing or browsing the Net it means checking out sites on the Internet. The Internet contains a graphical, easy to use system that offers vast amount of information. This system is called the World Wide Web (www) or Web. It consists of huge collection of pages containing information, images, sounds and video clips stored in computers around the world. Each page on a www is called a Webpage. The site which stores Web pages is called a Website. The first page of any website is called the Home Page. Various universities, companies etc have their own websites which contain several WebPages of information about the services they provide.

**Browsing the World Wide Web**

Each web page on the web has a unique address. This address is called URL (Uniform Resource Locator). The URLs of web pages start with **http://** where http stands for Hyper Text Transfer Protocol. To view a particular website, you will have to write the address or URL of that website in the Address bar of the web browser you are using.

**Creating an Email Account**

Once you are connected to the web, you can browse through the various sites, download programs and files, listen to music, chat with your friends or access any information that you need etc. Besides, you can also create an E-mail account, which is the most popular aspect of the web. Almost all the sites offer a free E-mail facility. You can access the free E-mail facility in any site that you find appropriate. Just click the button mentioned for a new user to sign up. A registration form will appear which should be filled up and submitted. Once accepted, you have your own E-mail account. After creating your account you can send mails to anyone in the world from your computer. And you can do so in the matter of a few seconds. The gmail New Account Sign up button and registration form is shown below. Follow the steps in the simulation session typing required information until the prompt Registration is complete to close the Internet Explorer, mo window.

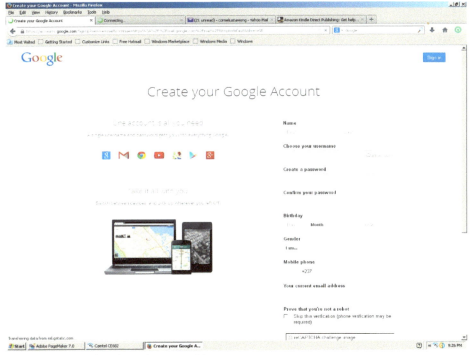

## Sign in and Check Emails

To sign in means to access a computer network by identifying oneself with a username and password. Make sure that the computer is connected to the Internet. Start any Internet Browser e.g. Internet explorer, Mozilla Firefox etc. Enter the following address in the browser's address field and press the Enter key on your keyboard:http://www.hotmail.com/

The Hotmail home page appears in the browser. In order to sign in to your hotmail account, enter your hotmail ID and Password, then click Sign in. Your personal hotmail welcome page now appears in the browser and shows you the number of new mails you have in your box. In order to see the senders of the mails as well as the dates of delivery, click on the **Inbox** folder and the Inbox page will open. In order to open and read emails, click the message's subject in the subject column. The message opens in the browser where you can read it, reply it, or forward it. To send emails, Click on compose button. The compose page is where you write and send emails. Click in the **To field**, and enter the email address of the person to whom the mail is intended. Click on the **Subject field** and enter the title or heading of the mail. Finally, click in the large text area and enter the message to be sent. After that, click the **Send** button.

To sign out means to discontinue access to the computer network that requires user identification. After checking, composing, sending or forwarding your emails, you can close your account. To do so, click on **sign out.**

**Managing the Mailbox**

A mailbox is a folder in which emails are stored. The four special purpose and permanent folders with a mail account are the Inbox, Draft, Sent, Trash and Bulk folders. The bulk is created when the first spam is received.

**Inbox:** All incoming messages (except suspected spam) appear in your inbox folder. You can read your emails in the Inbox, then delete them, move them to another folder, or leave them in the Inbox.

**Draft:** The Draft folder stores messages that you have composed but have not yet sent. A message that you save in your Draft folder remains there until you either send it or delete it.

**Sent:** You have the option of saving copies of the email message you send in the Sent folder. This makes it easy for you to review or resend the message, if the need arises.

**Trash:** When you delete messages, they are moved to the Trash folder. The mail server can delete messages in your Trash folder at any time without warning. You can also empty the Trash folder yourself.

**Bulk:** The first time you receive messages that the SpamGuard utility identifies as junk mail, it creates an additional folder called Bulk, where it stores these messages.

## Sending an Email with Attachment File

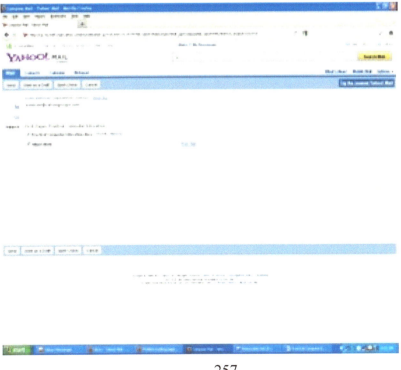

First, you need to select the file from a particular location (folder or drive) on your computer for attaching with the email message. For doing so, every website provides an option which allows you to browse your computer from your email account and select the file as an attachment. Once you have selected the file, the next task is attaching it with the email message. Once the file is attached, the website asks for confirmation. If you are sure about the attachment, you need to confirm it by clicking the button captioned as OK, Yes or Confirm Attachment. After attachment process is over, all you have to do is simply send the email to the intended recipient.

If your file, picture, book, movie or music is larger than 25MB the maximum size which yahoomail supports, to send as an attachment you can subscribe with www.sendthisfile.com or other websites which send larger capacity file attachments. www.sendthisfile.com is shown below.

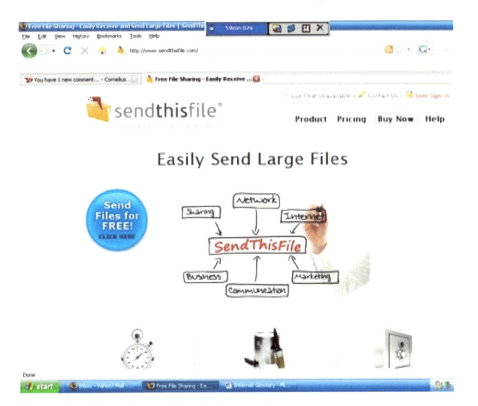

## Downloading from the Internet

You can get any information and lot of software free of charge from the Internet. All you have to do is simply locate the website providing the required information or software. But you may ask how to save the information or software available on the Internet on your computer. The answer to this question is: go for download. In the Internet context, term download means transferring some information or data from the Internet to your PC. Various websites, like www.download.com provides valuable information for free download.

## Facebook

Facebook is a social utility that connects people with friends and others. Facebook users must register before using the site. Additionally, users may join common-interest user groups, organized by workplace, school or college, or other characteristics. Users can create profiles with photos, lists of personal interests, contact information, and other personal information. Users can communicate with friends and other users through private or public messages and a chat feature. They can also create and join interest groups and "like pages" called "fan pages", some of which are maintained by organizations as a means of advertising.

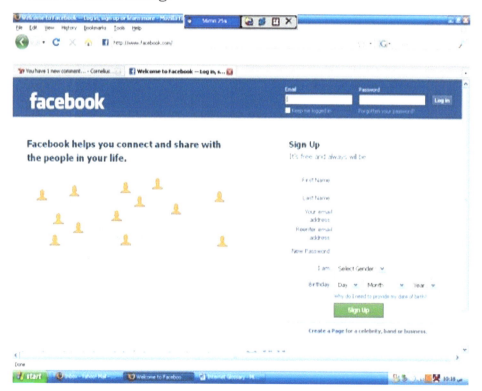

## Computer Viruses

Computer virus is a self–replicating piece of computer code that can partially or fully attach itself to computer files or applications. Like any other program, it contains instructions that tell your computer what to do. But unlike an application, a virus usually tells your computer to do something you don't want it to do. Computer viruses are the common cold of modern technology. They can spread swiftly across open networks such as the Internet, causing crores of rupees worth damage in a short span of time. If you are lucky, a virus will execute only a benign "personality quirk", such as causing your computer to make seemingly random beeps. But some viruses can be very destructive; they can format your hard drive, overwrite your hard drive boot sector, or delete files and render your machine inoperable.

· Viruses enter your system via email, downloads, infected flash and floppy disks, or (occasionally) hacking. By definition, a virus must be able to self – replicate (make copies of itself) to spread.

· Thousands of viruses exist, but few are found roaming, unchecked, across

networks.

· Virus behaviour can range from annoying to destructive. Sometimes

even relatively benign viruses tend to be destructive due to bugs introduced by sloppy programming.

Antivirus software can detect nearly all types of known viruses, but it must be updated regularly to maintain effectiveness.

## Symptoms of a Virus Attack

Some common symptoms of a virus attack are as follows:

· The computer begins to run slowly.

· Unusual messages and graphics appear on your screen for inexplicable

reasons.

· Music, not associated with any of the current programs, begins to play.

· Some of the program and/or data files have either been corrupted or

become difficult to locate.

· Unknown files or sub directories have been created.

· The sizes/dates of executable files change automatically.

· The computer does not remember the CMOS settings.

· The disk volume label has been changed mysteriously.

· The sizes of total and free memory are changed unexpectedly.

· The hardware devices begin to exhibit unusual behaviour.

## Antivirus Programs

Scanning programs installed on your computer to look for viruses (known and unknown ones) and remove from your computer. If it cannot remove it will quarantine the virus. Quarantine means keeping the virus in some isolated place on your computer under strict vigilance so that it could not do further harm to your computer. You can also delete detected viruses from your computer.

Viruses spread slowly and via the internet, floppy disks, flash memories CDs, DVDS shared between computers. Email viruses today account for more than 80 percent of virus infections and can infect thousands of machines in a matter of minutes.

You get a virus when you copy virus infected application or files to your computer. The virus code inside the infection application or file gets activated when you run the application or open the file. Once you open an infected file or application, the malicious code copies itself into a file on your computer, where it waits to start replicating.

## Types of Viruses

While there are thousands of virus variations, most fall into one of the following six general categories, each of which works its magic slightly differently:

Boot Sector Virus: It replaces or implants itself in the boot sector—an area of the hard drive (or any other disk) accessed first when you turn on your computer. This kind of virus can prevent you from booting your hard disk.

**File Virus**: It infects applications. The infected applications spread the virus by infecting associated documents and other applications whenever they're opened or run.

**Macro Virus**: Written using a simplified macro programming language, these viruses affect Microsoft Office applications, such as Word and Excel. This virus type accounts for about 75 percent of viruses found in the wild. A document infected with a macro virus generally modifies a pre-existing, commonly used command (such as Save) to trigger its payload upon execution of that command.

**Multipartite Virus**: It infects both files and the boot sector—a double whammy that can re-infect your system dozens of times before it is caught.

**Polymorphic Virus**: It changes code whenever it passes to another machine. In theory, these viruses should be more difficult for antivirus scanners to detect, but in practice they're usually not that well written.

**Stealth Virus**: It hides its presence by making an infected file not appear infected. However, it doesn't usually stand up to antivirus software.

**Worm**: Like a virus, is a program that harms the computer and destroys data stored in it.

**Trojan horse:** Is a program in which malicious or harmful code is contained inside apparently harmless programming or data in such a way that it can get control and do its chosen form of damage. Trojan horses unlike viruses do not replicate themselves but are destructive.

# Conclusion

You have come to the end of your course with Practical Computer Education. Hope you have enjoyed the work in this book. For you, it may be just a beginning. But, your newly acquired computer skills will go a long way in helping you improve your performance, no matter whatever field you are connected with. In this course, I have tried my best to acquaint you thoroughly with most aspects of Microsoft Windows, Microsoft Word and the Internet. Hope you have also enriched your practical knowledge.

With Cameroon hoping to become an emerging nation by 2035, the skills that you have learnt from this book will stand you in good opening in all your pursuits in this country. They will equip you with confidence and the extra edge that is essential for excelling in the job market different from just 'big' certificates without practical know how from schools. It will also help students who will in future study computer engineering to research more in their fields. Finally, I wish you a successful and prosperous future. Good Luck!

## Internet Glossary

**Blocking software** Computer programs that filter content from the Internet and block access to some Web sites or content based on specified criteria. Parents, teachers, or caregivers can use blocking software to prevent access to certain Web sites and other information available over the Internet.

**Blog** Short for Web log. A blog is a Web site to which one or more people post their personal observations on particular subjects.

**Bookmark** A file within a browser in which an Internet user can save the addresses of interesting or frequently used Web sites, so that they are readily available for re-use.

**Cache** A file on the hard drive in which a Web browser stores information such as addresses, text, and graphics from recently visited Web sites, making it easier and faster for the user to revisit a site.

**Chat** A feature offered by many online services or Web sites that allows participants to "chat" by typing messages which are displayed almost instantly on the screens of other participants who are using the chat room.

**Chat room** The name given to a place or page in a Web site or online service where people can "chat" with each other by typing messages which are displayed almost instantly on the screens of others who are in the "chat room." Chat rooms are also called "online forums."

**Cookie** A piece of information sent by a Web server to a user's browser.

**Default** a setting automatically chosen by a program or machine that remains until the user specifies another setting.

**Discussion group** Online area, like an electronic bulletin board, where users can read and add or "post" comments about a specific topic. Users can find discussion groups, also referred to as "discussion boards," for almost any topic.

**Download** to transfer (copy) files from one computer to another. "Download" can also mean viewing a Web site, or material on a Web server, with a Web browser.

266

**E-mail** (Electronic Mail) –Messages sent through an electronic (computer) network to specific groups or individuals. Though e-mail is generally text, users can attach files that include graphics, sound, and video.

**Email Header** Information that identifies the sender and recipient of a message, information about how the message was routed through the network, the date and time at which the message was sent, and the subject of the message.

**Encryption** A means of making data unreadable to everyone except the recipient of a message. Encryption is often used to make the transmission of credit card numbers secure for those who are shopping on the Internet.

**Executable file** A file that is in a format the computer can directly execute, as opposed to source files, which are created by and for the user. Executable files are essential to running your computer, but can also do it harm. Spyware programs often include executable files that can operate without your knowledge.

**File Sharing** Accessing files on one computer from a different computer

**Firewall** Hardware or software that secures computer files by blocking unauthorized access. Many computers already have them, but they must be activated by the user.

**FTP** (File Transfer Protocol) –A way of transferring files over the Internet from one computer to another.

**Hacker** Someone who breaks into your computer (or into a network of computers) over the Internet.

**Hidden dialers** Programs that are often unwittingly downloaded that will use your computer to silently dial expensive phone calls which show up on your phone bill.

**Home page** The first page on a Web site, which introduces the site and provides the means of navigation.

**HTML**(Hypertext Markup Language) –The coded format language used for creating hypertext documents on the World Wide Web and controlling how Web pages appear.

**HTTP** (Hypertext Transfer Protocol) –The standard language that computers connected to the World Wide Web use to communicate with each other.

**Hyperlink** An image or portion of text on a Web page that is linked to another Web page, either on the same site or in another Web site. Clicking on the link will take the user to another Web page, or to another place on the same page. Words or phrases which serve as links are underlined, or appear in a different colour, or both. Images that serve as links have a border around them, or they change the cursor to a little hand as it passes over them. **Internet** – A global connection of computer networks.

**Intranet** A private network inside a company or organization, which uses software like that used on the Internet, but is for internal use only, and is not accessible to the public.

**IP** (Internet Protocol) The computer language that allows computer programs to communicate over the Internet.

**IP Address** (or IP number) – A set of four numbers, each between zero and 255, separated by periods (eg: 192.168.0.5). The IP address uniquely identifies a computer or other hardware device (such as a printer) on the Internet.

**ISP** (Internet Service Provider) – A company that sells direct access to the Internet, most often through dialing a local phone number. Unlike some online services, ISPs provide little or no proprietary content or online services.

**Keyword** A word that is entered into the search form or search "window" of an Internet search engine to search the Web for pages or sites about or including the keyword and information related to it.

**Kids' Web Sites** Web sites designed for children under 13 years old, or which attract visitors who are under 13.

**LAN** Local Area Network –A network of connected computers that are generally located near each other, such as in an office or company.

**Link** A word, phrase, or image highlighted in a hypertext document to act as a navigation aid to related information. Links may be indicated with an underline, a colour contrast, or a border.

**Mailing list** An E-mail-based discussion forum dedicated to a topic of interest. An interested Internet user can subscribe to a mailing list by sending an e-mail message that contains appropriate instructions to a specific e-mail address.

**Modem** A hardware device that allows computers to communicate with each other by transmitting signals over telephone lines, enabling what is called "dial-up access."

**Monitoring software** Software products that allow a parent or caregiver to monitor or track the Web sites or e-mail messages that a child visits or reads, without necessarily blocking access.

**Multimedia** Information presented in more than one format, such as text, audio, video, graphics, and images.

**Navigation** A system of hypertext paths set up on a Web page to enable visitors to find their way around the site.

**Netiquette** The informal rules of Internet courtesy, enforced exclusively by other Internet users.

**Newsgroups** Discussion groups on the Internet.

**Operating System** The main program that runs on a computer. An operating system allows other software to run and prevents unauthorized users from accessing the system. Major operating system include UNIX, Windows, MacOS, and Linux.

**Persistent Cookies** Cookies that are discarded when they reach their defined expiration time.

**Phishing** An identity theft scam in which criminals send out spam that imitates the look and language of legitimate correspondence from e-commerce sites. The fake messages generally link to Web sites which are similarly faked to look like the sites of the respected companies.

**Plug-in** A small piece of software that enriches a larger piece of software by adding features or functions. Plug-ins enable browsers to play audio and video.

**Posting** Sending a message to a discussion group or other public message area on the Internet. The message itself is called a "post."

**Public Forums** Refers to digital entities such as bulletin boards, public directories, or commercial CD-ROM directories, where personal user data may be distributed by a site or a service provider.

**Search engine** A tool that enables users to locate information on the World Wide Web. Search engines use keywords entered by users to find Web sites which contain the information sought. Some search engines are specifically designed to find Web sites intended for children.

**Server** A special computer connected to a network that provides (serves up) data. A Web server transmits Web pages over the Internet when it receives a Web browser's request for a page. A server can also be called a host or node.

**Session Cookies** Cookies that do not have a specific expiration time and are discarded when Internet Explorer 6.0 is closed.

**Spam** Unsolicited "junk" e-mail sent to large numbers of people to promote products or services. Sexually explicit unsolicited e-mail is called "porn spam." Also refers to inappropriate promotional or commercial postings to discussion groups or bulletin boards.

**Subscription Data** Subscription data is the information that you provide to an online service when you sign up to become a member.

**Surf** To search for information on the Web in a random, non-linear way.

**TCP/IP** (Transmission Control Protocol / Internet Protocol) –The protocols, or conventions, that computers use to communicate over the Internet.

**Trojans** Programs designed to allow third parties unauthorized access to the computer systems they infect. Trojans may also be used in order to exploit a computer system to send unsolicited email.

**Uninstall** The process of removing a program from a computer. Some applications must be removed with an uninstall program, which removes all files that were installed with the program and restores any modifications made to system files.

**Unique email address** An address that is hard for spammers to guess, but easy for you to remember. For example, using both letters and numbers in your email address may make it difficult for spammers to guess your email address.

**Upload** Copying or sending files or data from one computer to another. A Web developer, for example, could upload a document to a Web server. (See also download)

**URL** (Uniform Resource Locator) –The World Wide Web address of a site on the Internet. The URL for the The Ministry of Secondary Education Cameroon, for example, is http://www.minesec.gov.cm (See also "Domain name")

**Virus** A program that is loaded onto your computer unbeknownst to you. Viruses can make copies of themselves, quickly using up all available memory. Some viruses can transmit themselves across networks.

**Web** The World Wide Web. An Internet system to distribute graphical, hyper-linked information, based on the hypertext transfer protocol (HTTP). The World Wide Web is also known as WWW or W3. The Web is not synonymous with the Internet; rather, it is just one service on the Internet. Other services on the Internet include Internet Relay Chat and Newsgroups. The Web is accessed through use of a browser.

**Web-based chat** Chat rooms that are found in Web sites, which allow people to chat with each other using their browsers. Another kind of chat room, Internet Relay Chat (IRC), requires additional software. (See also "Chat room," and "IRC")

**Web-based e-mail** A technology that allows users to send and receive e-mail using only a browser, rather than using an e-mail program such as Eudora.

**Web-based instant-messaging**
Instant-messaging technology that works in Web sites, as opposed to that provided by commercial online services. (See also "Instant messaging")

**Web site** A collection of "pages" or files linked together and available on the World Wide Web. Web sites are provided by companies, organizations and individuals.

**Webmaster** The person responsible for administering a Web site.

**Worm** A program that reproduces itself over a network, usually performing malicious actions, such as using up the computer's resources and possibly shutting the system down.

**WWW** The World Wide Web.

## Cameroon National Anthem

O Cameroon, Thou Cradle of our Fathers;

Holy Shrine where in our midst they now

repose,

Their tears and blood and sweat thy soil did

water,

On thy hills and valleys once their tillage rose

Dear Fatherland, thy worth no tongue can tell!

How can we ever pay thy due?

Thy welfare we will win in toil and love and

peace,

Will be to thy name ever true!

### Chorus:

Land of Promise, Land of Glory!

Thou, of life and joy, our only Store!

Thine be honour, thine devotion,

And deep endearment, for evermore.

From Shari, from where the Mungo Meanders

From along the banks of lowly Boumba Stream,

Muster thy sons in union close around thee,

Mighty as the Buea Mountain be their team;

Instill in them the love of gentle ways,

Regret for errors of the past;

Foster, for Mother Africa, a loyalty
That true shall remain to the last.

www.ingramcontent.com/pod-product-compliance
Lightning Source LLC
LaVergne TN
LVHW012316070326
832902LV00004BA/73